Dealing with disruption in fostering and adoption placements

Hedi Argent and Jeffrey Coleman

Published by
British Association for Adoption & Fostering
(BAAF)
Saffron House
6–10 Kirby Street
London EC1N 8TS
www.baaf.org.uk

Charity Registration 275689 (England and Wales) and SC039337 (Scotland)

British Library Cataloguing in Publication Data
A catalogue record for this book is available from the British Library

ISBN 978 1 907585 53 1

Project management by Jo Francis, BAAF
Designed and typeset by Helen Joubert Design
Printed in Great Britain by the Lavenham Press

BAAF is the leading UK-wide membership organisation for all those concerned with adoption, fostering and child care issues.

Contents

Appendices

Acknowledgements

We are indebted to all our colleagues who have contributed their experience and expertise, especially to Marion Hundleby for her helpful comments on the original proposal, and to Pat Beesley, Sarah Borthwick, Cherry Harnott, Phillida Sawbridge and Chris Stansell for reading the almost final draft. Thanks also to Alexandra Plumtree, Deborah Cullen and Mary Romaine for their help with the chapter on the law.

We want to thank Shaila Shah, BAAF's Director of Publications, for her unfailing support.

This guide could only be produced because children, carers and social workers have generously shared the pain and narratives of disruption; we are grateful to all of them and hope that their experience will help other children, families and agencies.

The cases quoted in this book are based on fact, but names and situations have been changed to preserve anonymity.

Note about the authors

Hedi Argent is an independent adoption consultant, trainer and freelance writer.

She chairs disruption meetings for BAAF Southern England. She is the author of *Find me a Family* (Souvenir Press, 1984), *Whatever Happened to Adam?* (BAAF, 1998), *Related by Adoption* (BAAF, 2004), *One of the Family* (BAAF, 2005), *Josh and Jaz have Three Mums* (BAAF, 2007) and several titles in BAAF's Ten Top Tips series, the co-author of *Taking Extra Care* (BAAF, 1997) and the editor of *Keeping the Doors Open* (BAAF, 1988), *See you Soon* (BAAF, 1995), *Staying Connected* (BAAF, 2002) and *Models of Adoption Support* (BAAF, 2003). She has also contributed seven illustrated booklets to the children's guides series published by BAAF.

Jeffrey Coleman qualified as a social worker in 1977. He has had considerable experience as a social worker and manager in West London and has been Director of BAAF Southern England since 1999. He has been Chair of several adoption panels and chairs disruption meetings for BAAF. He was involved in developing the training pack *Parenting the Sexually Abused Child* (BAAF, 2004) and contributed to the anthology *Models of Adoption Support* (BAAF, 2003).

1 Introduction

This guide is concerned with children who move into permanent placements and then have to move again contrary to expectations. Many of them have complex histories of neglect and harm. According to the Oxford English Dictionary, disruption is the action of rending or bursting asunder, or a forcible severance. Disruption in families is not new. Some children and young people are rejected by their parents; some have to be removed from their homes because they were abused or neglected; some explode out of their families during a stormy adolescence; and a few are orphaned. Whichever way it happens, and for whatever reason, it is a disruption of the accepted and expected course of family life. For the purpose of this guide, **disruption is the premature ending of an adoption or "permanent" foster placement**. Much of what follows will also be relevant for time-limited and task-focused child care arrangements.

Disruptions can occur during introductions, and before or after a court order is made, whether it is for adoption, residence or special guardianship. When and how a placement disrupts will make a fundamental difference to the child, the prospective adopters, the birth family, and the agencies concerned. Depending on the timing of the disruption, the child may have to return to a pre-existing care situation or may have to be "looked after" by the local authority where the adopters live. It is, of course, always possible for a child to return to the family after what seems to be a disruption, and this may be the most positive outcome if adequate support is available. Residence, special guardianship and other orders can be varied or revoked by a court, but adoptions cannot be dissolved in the UK. The adopters are the legal parents, even if the child is subject to a care order or a supervision requirement, unless and until the child is adopted again. Potential permanent carers may therefore find themselves in a range of different circumstances after disruption: they may retain full parental responsibility or share it with the local authority; they could remain significant people in the child's life; or they may wish, or be expected, to disconnect from the child altogether. Agencies will have to make decisions about the child's best interests, which may include further family finding, family support and child protection.

The word "disruption", in preference to the more pejorative term "breakdown", was first used by Kay Donley to describe the unplanned ending of a family placement in the early 1970s. 'When there is a disruption, there is a family crisis,' said Donley at a seminar organised by BAAF in 1975. Donley was the director of a pioneering American adoption agency called Spaulding for Children. This agency led the way in finding permanent families for older and disabled children and promoted the idea that, when a placement cannot continue, it is not a breakdown but a disruption of the family placement process. It is perhaps appropriate to go further now, and to maintain that disruption is a part of that process and that awareness of disruption should be built into the training and preparation of prospective adopters and foster carers.

Recently in the US, it has been argued that avoiding negative terminology is important when so many children entering care following an adoption may return to their adoptive families. Festinger (2009) suggests (in a US context) that 'post-adoption placement should be preferred to the term "adoption displacement" to steer clear of labelling, and to ensure all possibilities, including a return to the placement, are considered following a child's removal from an adoptive home.'

Adoption social workers will include some discussion of disruption in their work with prospective carers, although it is never easy. Few of us like to sound a negative note so early on. But it is important that disruption risk is fully explored right from the beginning as part of an open and ongoing dialogue between adopters and agencies. After all, as Festinger (2005) says:

> *In view of the emotional baggage that children bring to a placement, the multiplicity of factors in the [new] home environment, and the flaws in our ability to predict their interaction, it is inevitable that some disruptions will occur. The point is that disruptions neither end the hope for, nor likelihood of, a later successful adoption. In the process, children, families, and workers can learn how to improve the chances that the next placement will hold.*

While adoption outcomes for children placed young are very good, and for later placed children still very much "worth the risk" (Rushton, 2003), some placements will disrupt. It should not be a matter of failing or succeeding as carers, but of being given the tools to manage, and the support to withdraw if and when it is no longer possible to manage.

But even where high standards of work in adoption practice, based on sensitivity and a commitment to open communication, are achieved by adopters and social workers, risk cannot be eliminated. A child may enter an adoptive placement having had insufficient time to mourn losses, key transitions may have been hurried by agency resource pressures, or his/her early adversities may still remain undisclosed or have eluded proper assessment. Coping with the anxiety of possible failure is inseparable from decision-making for vulnerable children. But a false expectation of a hundred per cent success rate will only intensify these feelings if placement difficulties arise.

Sudden tragedy can sometimes strike for an adoptive family, with major illness or the death of a carer destabilising the family supports for the child in placement. More often, disruption is not so event-specific in cause, and does not happen overnight. There is usually a process leading to disruption, even if it happens at an early stage or during introductions.

If carers and workers can work openly together, a final crisis may be averted. Whatever their difficulties, most adopters and foster carers have a keen sense of responsibility and are aware that yet another move may be extremely damaging for the child.

> *Disruptions were rarely precipitous. Most involved at least a year of difficulty; some lasted many years before deteriorating to the point of disruption. The typical family gave the agency little notice that the placement was heating up until the water was about to boil over.* (Barth and Berry, 1988, p.177)

2 Overview of disruption

In 1983, when John Fitzgerald wrote *Understanding Disruption* (BAAF 1983, 1990), disruption meetings were still rare, but when the second edition was published in 1990, he said, 'many agencies have started using the disruption meeting process as a matter of course'. Some agencies have extended this service to include disruptions in short-term foster care.

In *Learning from Disruption*, Sheila Smith (1994) points out that:

> *One of the consistently worrying aspects of disruption meetings is the paucity of information recorded on file about children's early lives and development (p.45)... Amid the domination exerted by adults' concerns, the child's response is lost. Records are often too adult-centred, often dominated by problems around relationships, violence, finance or child protection issues. It is so easy to lose sight of the child, and accurate observations about their development, play, attachments and routines are frequently absent.* (p.6)

OUTCOMES

> *The concept of outcome is fraught with difficulty. Success or otherwise of a placement depends on many factors, including whose perspective is taken and which objective is being examined, as well as when the outcome is being measured. Defining disruption – the extent to which placements remained intact was, in some cases, surprisingly difficult to define... Although in most cases disruptions were fairly clear cut, there were some young people living outside the family at the time of follow-up whose circumstances were ambiguous.* (Rushton and Dance, 2004, p.50)

Alan Rushton and Cherilyn Dance classified outcomes from the perspective of the family unit, according to whether the young person was treated as a continuing family member; understandably, they considered placements intact if young people currently out of the home were still viewed as family members.

Precise statistical details about disruption are not available. In December 2001, the Adoption and Permanence Team at the Department of Health

(DH, LAC (2001) 33) noted that current data collection did not allow for the recording of children returning to care as a result of disruption. It made a proposal to provide national estimates for England of the number of children adopted from care whose adoptions had broken down after the making of an adoption order, by including adoption breakdown on the statistical collection for looked after children (SSDA903 return). This has not as yet been implemented, and the proposal does not refer to disruptions before an order is made, or to the disruption of permanent foster placements. But there is an "official view".

"An official view"

Do many placements break down? Until recently, UK government websites quoted a 20 per cent disruption rate in adoption as a rough average. Currently, with adoption at the forefront of ministers' attention in England, there is a strong "official" emphasis on adoption and its stability, reflecting the many research studies in recent years that have found that long-term foster placements are more likely to disrupt than adoptive placements, though many children do settle and have successful outcomes in long-term foster care.

A recent study, titled *Belonging and Permanence* (Biehal *et al*, 2010), explored the outcomes of three placement options: adoption by "strangers", adoption by carers and longer-term foster care. The study found that 13 per cent of the children who had been placed for adoption or adopted at any point in their lives had been involved in an adoption disruption, compared with 28 per cent of fostered children who had left their foster carers after placements lasting three or more years. Furthermore, when a child was adopted quickly, before their first birthday, the disruption figure was about two or three per cent.

However, comparisons between the stability of adoption and long-term foster care are not straightforward. Children in long-term foster placements tend to enter placement at an older age than children being adopted, and previous research on adoption and foster care has identified a relationship between age at placement and disruption risk. The older the child at the time of placement, the higher the chance of the placement breaking down. Other risk factors can include the following:

- that the child had a history of behavioural/emotional difficulties;
- that the child had a history of abuse/neglect;
- that the child was placed separately from his or her brothers and sisters;
- attachment to birth family – see Quinton (2012).

WHAT RESEARCH TELLS US

> *Over the last 30 years, knowledge has accumulated from about a dozen adoption outcome studies to the effect that four out of five non-relative adoptions from care, in middle childhood, are likely to continue, at least through the early years.* (Rushton and Dance, 2004, p.49)

Broadly speaking, disruption studies of children placed after infancy confirm an average rate of 20 per cent, with a range of 10–50 per cent.

The Maudsley study (Rushton and Dance, 2004) of 133 late-placed adoption and foster care placements reported a disruption rate of eight per cent after one year and 29 per cent six years later. On average, placements disrupted 34 months after placement. About half the disruptions occurred despite parents feeling confident a year into the placement, and a similar number of placements endured even though parents had expressed significant worries a year into the placement.

From a Department of Health inspection overview in 2000, based on data supplied by local authorities on 1,952 children, it appeared that one in 10 placements disrupted in the very early stages, and the process of family finding had to begin all over again (DH, 2000).

Taken together, social science research studies on disruption during the 1980s and 1990s have estimated rates as being between 10 and 27 per cent. Most studies with high rates were reporting on small samples of "hard to place" children, usually meaning much older children, with rates generally declining through the 1990s. (See Appendix 1 for summary of survey findings.)

Ofsted's Annual Report in 2011 highlighted that the best adoption agencies examine the details of every adoption breakdown to determine whether any aspect of their processes could be improved.

Julie Selwyn and colleagues at the Hadley Centre at the University of Bristol were commissioned in early 2012 by the Department for Education to research disruption rates across England along with explanations and perspectives of the reasons and consequences of those disruptions. It is expected that the results of that research will become available from 2013 onwards.

Behavioural problems

The majority of disruptions occur because of high levels of behavioural problems usually accompanied by relationship difficulties between the child and adopters or foster carers. Attachment theory must therefore be considered as one of the building blocks of placement work (Howe *et al*, 1999).

Some behavioural problems linked to attachment difficulties may be unidentified at the start of the placement.

> *They [the social workers] just wanted him to have a family. They were desperate for this young lad to have a lovely family and lovely home and a nice mum and dad. But it doesn't work like that. He needed help. Love isn't enough. I feel a fool that I let it go on for as long as I did. I feel as though they took full advantage of us as a new foster family. I just hope that if they've got a very disturbed child in the future they think really carefully where the child will go.* (Quoted in Rushton and Dance, 2004, p.52)

However, it may not always be possible to know whether these characteristics are the cause or effect of a failing placement.

Preferential rejection

"Preferential rejection" refers to a specific form of emotional abuse that describes rejecting behaviour by a birth parent towards only one child in a sibling group. A significant relationship has been found between this kind of emotional abuse and poorer outcomes (Quinton *et al*, 1998; Dance *et al*, 2002). See Table 1 for the significantly increased risks associated with preferential rejection (Dance and Rushton, 2005).

For the categorical variables, this equates to at least a five-fold increase in odds of disruption for children who have experienced preferential rejection and an eight-fold increase where the adoptive mother perceives a lack of attachment by the child. Of the 13 children in this sample who had experienced preferential rejection, eight subsequently experienced disruption.

Table 1: Predictors of disruption versus continuing placement

		95% C.I. for O.R.		
Characteristic	**Odds ratio**	**Lower**	**Upper**	**Significance (P=)**
Age at placement (months)	1.07	1.02	1.12	.007
Preferential rejection	5.64	0.95	33.67	.058
Time in care (months)	1.04	1.00	1.07	.047
Level of behavioural problems and overactivity at 1 year (T2)	1.18	0.99	1.41	.061
Lack of attachment to mother at 1 year (T2)	8.79	1.93	40.12	.005

(From Dance and Rushton, 2005, p.277)

C.I., confidence interval; O.R., odds ratio

Several researchers have concluded that prior disruption history places a child at increased risk for a subsequent disruption (Evan B Donaldson Adoption Institute, 2004).

Sexual abuse history

Although a majority of children placed for adoption from the care system will have suffered serious abuse, it is not easy for researchers to link particular maltreatment to disrupted placements if case records do not give detailed accounts. Skilled practitioners and BAAF staff who chair disruption meetings are aware that a child's pre-placement experience of abuse significantly increases the risk of disruption, and children who have experienced sexual abuse may be particularly vulnerable in placement.

Smith and Howard's 1994 adoption study comparing 35 sexually abused children with 113 with no identified history of sexual abuse, found that the disruption rate was higher for the abused group than for the non-abused group. They also noted that sexual abuse was associated with more moves in care, greater behavioural difficulties, and more attachment problems or hostile acting out. Many of the children were not identified as having previously been victims of sexual abuse until long after their adoptive placements.

Pollock and Farmer's work (2005), exploring the needs of a sample of sexually abused and abusing children entering care, suggests the pervasive vulnerability of these abused children throughout the cycle of childhood. They had more difficulties in their early history than non-sexually abused children, because of the abuse itself and the neglectful and abusive context within which it occurred. They were more likely to have had a previous admission into the care system, and to have spent significantly longer in care, compared to other looked after children.

Sexual abuse may give rise to "multiple models" of parental behaviour, instead of a single coherent representation. For instance, where an abusing (or collusive) parent insists on a distorted account of traumatic events the child has actually observed or experienced, the effect is to create in the child victim a sense, albeit conflicted, of being specially loved or privileged by their "special" relationship with the abuser.

Suffering from multiple stresses, and an impaired capacity to recover from trauma, having profound unmet needs for good, secure parenting, and struggling with unresolved difficulties in their relationships with their birth families, these are children decidedly at long-term risk in terms of educational attainment, social functioning and disruption of fostering and adoption placements.

Exposure to pre-natal drug and alcohol misuse

There is no distinct correlation between parental drug and alcohol misuse and disruption of long-term placements.

> *It is still not possible to determine precisely which children will be affected by parental substance misuse and in what way...not all children pre-natally exposed to drugs and alcohol will have long-term problems [the spectrum will run from minimal to very severe].* (Mather, 2004, p.22)

This would suggest that regular monitoring could reduce the risk of future disruptive effects.

> *We had no idea what the effects of the birth mothers' drug and alcohol abuse would have on our child. [We needed to know] what services we might need in the future and where to seek them. Parents need help in many ways we can't imagine until it happens.* (Adopter in Howard and Smith, 2003, p.67)

Full information and expert preparation of prospective carers are essential.

> *In addition to the usual roles which all parents undertake, substitute carers have to uncover, discover or simply guess about the past and its continuing influence on the future of their child...No one should ever be asked to parent a child in the absence of any of the information that is available to professionals about the child...Foster and adoptive parents need to be archaeologists before they can be the architects of their children's future.* (Mather, 2004, p.22–23)

However, Barth and Brooks (2000), in a study of outcomes of 121 pre-natally drug-exposed children and 112 non-drug exposed children, eight years after adoption, found that drug-exposed children had only modestly more difficulties in general adjustment and behaviour, education and physical health than the others. They also found that the adoptive parents of the drug-exposed children had adequate understanding of the difficulties and appropriate expectations, and that their commitment to, and satisfaction with, their adoptions were as high as those of parents who adopted non-drug-exposed children.

Carers' expectations and experience

One of the more disquieting findings in the disruption literature is that more educated parents, particularly mothers, may be more likely to have troubled placements that are at greater risk of disruption (Boyne *et al*, 1984; Barth and Berry, 1988). Although Partridge *et al* (1986) did not find education significant in predicting disruption, the studies that did find a difference theorise that this could be in part because of the heightened expectations that more educated parents may have of their children, as well as the lack of community resources equipped to handle children with special needs (Barth and Berry, 1991). However, recent UK studies have not found the same association between educational status and outcomes. Perhaps the best conclusion here is that, as Quinton (2012) suggests, though not a risk as such, educational status may be an index of adopter behaviours and characteristics that will be problematic if they are a mismatch with the child's needs.

Howard and Smith's 2003 study showed that being fully prepared for adoption is the strongest parent-related factor for predicting positive child adjustment after adoption, though as Rosenthal (1993) noted, some parents harbour unrealistic expectations despite explicit preparation by social workers. Foster carers are in the best position to avoid unrealistic expectations of a child they are already caring for. A review of US research (Evan B. Donaldson Adoption Institute, 2004) suggests that: 'As many studies have found, adoption by foster parents consistently reduces the risk of adoption termination.'

SOCIAL AND PROFESSIONAL SUPPORT

Research has associated social support with placement stability. Rosenthal (1993) cited two studies showing that the support of family and friends, as well as religious communities, enhances stability. Leung and Erich (2002) cited several studies as evidence that support networks play a "vital" role in post-adoptive family functioning, and found in their own research that the higher the support from a spouse, other adoptive parents, physicians and day care centres, the higher the level of post-adoptive family functioning.

Berry (1997) reported that disruptions were more likely to occur in families with little social support and few contacts with relatives, and his findings showed that knowing other adoptive parents and foster carers was associated with stability. McRoy (1999) identified support systems, including family, friends, the church and outside community involvement, to be strengths associated with stability. This is echoed by Erich and Leung's (1998) long-term outcome analysis of intact placements; family functioning scores were significantly higher when the mother participated in religious activities.

> *In view of the finding that social workers almost never had contact with anyone in the families' support networks, adoption workers may do well to reduce the emphasis on personal information of applicants, and instead focus on assessing, building, and enlisting familial and social support for the placement.* (Barth and Berry, 1988, p.128)

In Barth and Berry's 1988 research, expectations and use of support services varied greatly.

> *Help-seeking patterns differed dramatically for stable and disrupted placements. Almost one-half of disrupted placements did not report seeking help from any source and 43 per cent reported seeking professional services. The stable placements, on the other hand, rarely reported seeking no help (9 per cent) and more often used professional assistance (60 per cent).* (p.149)

Families where placements disrupted sought the agency's help later than families where placements proved stable.

A range of other factors has been identified as influential in placement outcome including maternal age and employment, and the role of birth children, but the failure to replicate these over different studies suggests that they may be an artefact of either the sampling or the research design. A number of factors have *not* proved to be associated consistently with outcome, namely the sex and ethnicity of the child and the previous parenting experience of the adopters, although many practitioners firmly believe that the lack of parenting experience of troubled children increases the risk of disruption.

As we have seen, research can direct our attention to a number of risk factors that may increase the probability of disruption in any particular case. But to what extent can these risks be counter-balanced by well-focused social work practice? Unfortunately, disruptions are still not nationally or comprehensively tracked to enable reliable messages for practice to emerge. But the small-scale studies and surveys completed to date can surely guide us into improving practice outcomes. (A detailed discussion of the factors leading to disruption follows in Chapter 4.)

3 The legal framework

This guide focuses on disruptions of agency adoptions, i.e. cases involving children relinquished by their mother at birth, and children in the care system who cannot live within their own families.

DISRUPTION AND THE LAW

Until recently there was no specific mention of adoption disruption in UK legislation. In England and Wales, before the Adoption and Children Act 2002, the legal framework for adoption services had been contained in the Adoption Act 1976. However, apart from financial support, the 1976 Act did not specify what needed to be provided in terms of adoption support and did not refer to disruption.

In Scotland, prior to the Adoption and Children (Scotland) Act 2007, the concept of a need for adoption support was established in Section 1 of the Adoption (Scotland) Act 1978. The duties that were set out at that time required every local authority adoption agency to have support services for a range of people, including children who were or may be adopted, and adopters. This would be interpreted as including situations relating to disruption although, as in other parts of the UK, this was not specifically mentioned.

In Northern Ireland, while adoption legislation does not refer to disruption, the 2010 Adoption Regional Policies and Procedures outline the process to be followed in the event that a placement for adoption ends prematurely prior to an adoption order being granted. Legislative reform in adoption currently awaited is likely to include specific reference to adoption disruption and the support needs of both the child and the adoptive family.

THE NEED FOR CHANGE

This very loose legal framework for adoption support affected the practice of dealing with disruption. A frequent criticism, underpinned by evidence from government inspections, was that services were inconsistent and patchy, with many authorities confining themselves to making very limited arrangements. By the 1990s, researchers were increasingly highlighting the stresses children and adopters faced if services were not available when a placement ended prematurely. Describing adoptive parents they had met where placements had disrupted, Lowe and Murch *et al* (1999) wrote:

> *The emotional pain, anxiety, exhaustion and, sometimes, financial expense associated with disruption, were all too obvious when we interviewed them (p. 216)...Although disruption meetings are considered desirable by agencies, they are not standard practice. Meetings were held in only two of the five cases in our sample.* (p. 236)

Few would have disagreed when the Department of Health consultation document, *Providing Effective Adoption Support*, issued in June 2002, stressed the lack of clarity surrounding services for disruption, and cited evidence of the need for greater investment. The document argued that it was important that such services were in place and known about by adoptive families to prevent unnecessary stress, and avoidable disruptions. The passage into law of the Adoption and Children Act 2002 provided the opportunity to modernise the whole framework for adoption support services in England and Wales, including services for disruption.

ENGLAND AND WALES

The Children Act 1989

It should be noted that, in England and Wales, children placed for adoption or where there is 'authority to place' are still looked after under the Children Act 1989. Therefore, until the making of an adoption order the local authority will still have the responsibilities set out in Part III of the 1989 Act. These responsibilities are supplemented and modified by the Adoption Agencies Regulations 2005.

The Adoption and Children Act 2002

The Adoption and Children Act 2002, and its accompanying regulations, include certain specific requirements about adoption support services and disruption.

The Act makes clear that any decisions relating to the adoption of a child must give paramount consideration to the welfare of the child throughout life, and the Welfare Checklist in section 1 of the Act sets out matters that must be taken into account. Decisions to be taken about a child whose adoption or adoptive placement has disrupted, however, may or may not be 'decisions relating to adoption'. Where the decision is not one 'relating to adoption' but the child is looked after by the local authority, the ordinary duty in section 22 of the Children Act 1989 to safeguard and promote the child's welfare will apply. The following explicit duties of agencies in relation to disruption must be seen within the overall framework of the Adoption and Children Act 2002 and the Children Act 1989.

Duties for agencies in England relating to disruption following the implementation of the 2002 Act on 30 December 2005 include the following.

Adoption Agencies Regulations 2005 (England)

Regulation 36 (10) – reviewing requirement after disruption:

Where the placement disrupts and the child is returned to the agency in accordance with section 35(1) or (2) of the Act, regulation 36 (10) of the Adoption Agencies Regulations 2005 now requires that:

> *'... the agency must conduct a review of the child's case no earlier than 28 days, or later than 42 days, after the date on which the child is returned to the agency, and when carrying out that review the agency must consider the matters set out in paragraph (6) (a), (b), (c) and (f)'.*

In effect, the agency should consider the full range of issues that may affect the child, and the following matters must be considered at the review:

(a) whether the adoption agency remains satisfied that the child should be placed for adoption;

(b) the child's needs, welfare and development, and whether any changes need to be made to meet his needs or assist his development;

(c) the existing arrangements for contact, and whether they should continue or be altered;

(d) in consultation with the appropriate agencies, the arrangements for assessing and meeting the child's health care and educational needs.

The agency should also consider its own decisions and actions in the case.

This is a formal reviewing requirement and runs alongside but is separate from the process of arranging a disruption meeting.

Adoption Support Services Regulations 2005 (England)

The Adoption Support Services Regulations 2005 (ASR) came into effect on 30 December 2005 and replaced the Adoption Support Services Regulations 2003 for England.

It is important to note that ensuring support in cases of disruption is now required by regulation 3(1) (f) of the ASR (for England) and that this is a new adoption support provision, which includes intercountry placements. The following are prescribed adoption support services:

> *(f) Assistance where disruption of an adoptive placement or adoption arrangement following the making of an adoption order has occurred, or is in danger of occurring, including:*
>
> *(i) making arrangements for the provision of mediation services and*
>
> *(ii) organising and running meetings to discuss disruptions in such placements or arrangements (ASR 3.1.f).*

Although there is no equivalent statutory requirement to deal with disruption in foster care, good practice would indicate that the same processes should be followed.

The Adoption Agencies Regulations 2005 (Wales)

Regulation 37 (11) – reviewing requirement after disruption:

> *(11) Where the child is returned to the adoption agency in accordance with section 35(1) or (2) of the Act, the agency must conduct a review of the child's case as soon as reasonably practicable and in any event no later than 28 days after the date on which the child is returned to the agency.*

It is important to note that ensuring support in cases of disruption is now required by regulation 3(1) (9e) and (f) of the Adoption Support Services (Local Authorities) (Wales) Regulations and that this is defined as an adoption support service by regulation 2(2)(d).

The Adoption Support Services (Local Authorities) (Wales) Regulations 2005

Section 3 requires that the following be provided:

> *(e) assistance for the purpose of ensuring the continuance of the relationship between the child and the child's adoptive parent, including –*
>
> *(i) training for adoptive parents for thepurpose of meeting any special needs of the child; and*
>
> *(ii) respite care; and*
>
> *(f) assistance where disruption of an adoption placement has occurred or is in danger of occurring including –*
>
> *(i) mediation; and*
>
> *(ii) organising and holding meetings to discuss disruptions in adoption placements.*

SCOTLAND

Adoption legislation in Scotland was updated by the Adoption and Children Act 2007 which was followed both by various regulations relating to adoption, and also by updated regulations about looked after children, including the provision of foster and kinship care. Although none of these directly address disruption – the focus is on positive improvement in planning and supporting permanence – they do make some relevant changes.

The new legal order introduced in the 2007 legislation is the permanence order (PO). Where this is intended to underpin permanent fostering arrangements, it replaces the former parental responsibilities order (PRO). It aims to be more flexible so that birth parents do not necessarily lose all their parental rights and foster carers may take on some responsibilities and rights through the ancillary provisions. As this is a recent order, it remains to be seen how the distribution of rights and responsibilities that suited a particular placement can best be renegotiated if it disrupts.

The Looked After Children (Scotland) Regulations 2009, in considering the frequency of children's reviews, allow flexibility in this respect for children placed on a PO, indicating that the local authority should agree the frequency of reviews with the child, depending on their age and maturity, and with the person caring for the child. Alternatively, if no such agreement is reached, after the first review at six weeks, subsequent reviews should be within 12 months of the previous review. The positive aim of this is to use a lighter touch where children are well settled in a permanent foster home. This may need to be reconsidered where a placement is struggling and a disruption is possible.

The other explicit purpose of a permanence order is when there is also a request to the court for authority to place the child for adoption. This is referred to as a permanence order with authority for adoption (POA), and replaces the freeing order. Until they are adopted, a child on a POA remains looked after in terms of Section 17(6) of the Children (Scotland) Act 1995, with all the duties that accompany this, including reviews. The relevant local authority must also hold one mandatory responsibility and one mandatory right for all children subject to a PO, including a POA. The mandatory right is that of deciding where the child should live. This offers much clearer local authority accountability for the welfare of children during the period before they are adopted than existed under the freeing provisions.

The other main thrust of the 2007 legislation was to strengthen the provision of adoption support services. This laid out in the Adoption Support Services and Allowances (Scotland) Regulations 2009 the rights of a whole range of people for such services and added a framework for seeking an assessment and the preparation of an adoption support plan. It does not, however, specifically refer to disruption. There is provision for termination of an adoption allowance if the adopted child ceases to have a home with an adoptive parent, unless its continuation is necessary for the needs of the child or there are exceptional circumstances. The Adoption Agencies (Scotland) Regulations 2009 include provision for a review of adopters without request either where no child has been placed within two years of their approval or where a child has been placed, no application for an adoption order has been made and 'the adoption agency considers that review of the prospective adopter's approval is necessary or appropriate to safeguard or promote the welfare of the child'. If, following such a review, the agency considers the prospective adopter is no longer suitable to be an adoptive parent, they must be referred to the adoption panel.

The 2007 Act also made an amendment to Section 11 of the Children (Scotland) Act 1995. This section is part of private law and allows various people to apply for some parental rights, the main ones being contact or residence. The 1995 Act specifically prohibited its use by birth parents who had lost their parental rights through orders such as adoption, freeing or a PRO. The 2007 amendment changed this to a restriction rather than a prohibition. Birth parents can now make an application under Section 11 but only for a contact order and must have the leave of the court to go ahead with a full application. While it remains to be seen how this will work in practice, there may be some situations when an adoption disrupts after a long period where some role for a birth parent may be beneficial for a child.

NORTHERN IRELAND

The Adoption (Northern Ireland) Order 1987 outlines the responsibilities of Health and Social Care Trusts to establish a support service for all those affected by adoption, including children who have been or may be adopted and anyone who has or may adopt a child. Adoption support may involve counselling and therapeutic services for both the child and their adoptive parents, including following a disruption. Where it becomes necessary for an adopted child to become looked after, the Children (Northern Ireland) Order Regulations and Guidance 1995 require local Health and Social Care Trusts to 'safeguard and promote the welfare of the child and in doing so to give consideration to the wishes and feelings of both the child and their parents'.

Where a disruption occurs before an adoption order is granted, the 2010 Adoption Regional Policies and Procedures outline the requirement for agencies to hold a disruption meeting and to review the prospective adopters.

4

Factors leading to disruption

Disruption is never the result of what one party has done or left undone. It is usually a combination of:

- unidentified circumstances
  (often known to different people involved, but not gathered together and brought into focus);
- misinterpreted circumstances
  (when pressures of deadlines and aspirations to achieve permanence for a child override careful evaluation of facts);
- unpredictable circumstances
  (situations or interactions that could not have been foretold by families or workers).

(Donley, 1981)

Families and children have to know from the beginning that, in spite of the most careful preparation, training, assessments, experience and knowledge, it is not possible to anticipate exactly what will happen when this child is placed with this family. Often we stand by and watch in respectful admiration as children and substitute parents, with incalculable effort and patience, make the most potentially problematic placements last. But together with the child and the carers, we also have to survive while seemingly promising foster and adoption placements crumble.

COMMON CAUSES OF DISRUPTION

- **Key information is incomplete or unshared** about the prospective carers or about the children and their birth families – possibly due to a well-intentioned but misguided attempt to present a positive picture and to avoid raising painful issues. Relevant facts can be withheld or missed.

  If a child's history and memory are contained in children's services' records, then it is not acceptable that the social workers for the child, or for the prospective family for that child, do not have the time to read them.

One prospective adopter at a disruption meeting complained about the child's profile featured in a magazine. It was written that Jamie was good at dancing, riding his bike and roller-skating, and that he liked to draw – activities that would fit in well with the adopters' lifestyle. In actual fact, Jamie's dancing seemed to be highly sexualised, he could not roller-skate or ride a bike unaided and he hated to draw. He said he was made to draw by his previous carers. The social worker who wrote the profile did not know Jamie and had accepted unverified information.

It can be tempting for us to ask children what kind of family they want and what they like to do, rather than to get to know the child: their concerns and fears, their understanding of family life, and the impact their experiences have had on their ability to convey their true wishes and feelings.

> *Workers believe they have communicated essential information, but it was ignored...Parents believe essential information was not given. Sometimes essential information was given but in such a way that it was not successfully communicated. For information to be successfully communicated, it must be both given and received.* (Donley Zeigler, 1996)

- **Inaccurate assessments of children's attachment patterns**, including attachments to foster carers, continuity needs, the effects of infant trauma and the failure to anticipate the relevance of the prospective carers' life history and lifestyle to the experiences of specific children.

It seems important to try to imagine the "internal picture" of parents that a maltreated child is likely to carry into a long-term placement.

Case example

Amanda's birth mother was unable to nurture and protect her effectively from birth, and eventually gave up. The vacuum was filled by her father, but he sexually abused her. Amanda's survival strategy involved identifying with her father, despite her fear of abuse. She may have seen him as strong and in control, possibly affectionate, providing some care, and offering her a special "privileged" position. Her mother appeared, by contrast, as rejecting and weak, to be treated only with contempt. Although not aware of it, in her adoptive placement she tried to "see off" the mother and sibling rivals, as the only way of securing some kind of security and power. Letting go of these distorted relationship patterns was always going to be difficult for her, but a clearer assessment of them might at least have helped the adopters to understand what was happening. The placement disrupted within a few months, after Amanda showed frightening aggression towards her adoptive mother and sister, while trying to share secrets with her father.

If a sexual abuse history is known or can be reasonably suspected before a child's placement, adopters should receive appropriate preparation and guaranteed access to services. There will be children with complex and perhaps not fully documented abuse histories where the possibility of past sexual abuse needs to be held in mind and inform work with the child within an adoption support plan (Hodges *et al*, 2003).

- The impact of **changes in the family** such as sickness, death, divorce, pregnancy, or redundancy on adoption support needs.
- **Post-adoption depression**, like post-natal depression, can be a seriously debilitating condition, which may be masked by more obvious problems in a placement.
- **Failure of therapeutic, health and education services** to meet an expected need, usually when transfer arrangements have not been completed before placement. It is beguiling to imagine that education and health care will eventually sort themselves out if the placement is right, but unsuitable schools, lack of specialist medical attention and waiting lists for therapy have caused many placements to falter, and eventually to disrupt.
- **Poor inter-agency and inter-departmental communication** – reading each other's files, sharing all information, establishing open lines of communication and clearly delineating tasks will avoid confusion not only for the workers but also for the child and the family.

  There were people coming in and out, telling us different things and giving us different advice – we never truly knew who was doing what and I don't think they did either. It was like the right hand not knowing what the left was doing. (Prospective adopter at disruption meeting)

- **Not enough support** for the foster carers to enable the child to move.

  He'd been with us for nearly two years and on the one hand we wanted him to have his own family but we didn't want to lose him altogether and in the end the social workers blamed us for giving him the wrong messages. (Foster carer at disruption meeting)

- **An adult agenda rather than a child-centred introduction plan**. It is surprising how often introductions are planned to fit in with pre-booked holidays, family events, time off, Christmas, travel convenience and financial considerations, rather than the needs and timescales of the child.
- **Not enough consideration of carers' own children's needs and perspectives**. One interview with the children is not enough.
- **Lack of clarity and agreement about both the purpose and management of contact**. Too often, contact arrangements are decided hastily pre-placement without including the prospective carers, and

without due consideration of all the child's meaningful connections and ways to ensure continuity.

- **Inadequate placement support**. Support is only as good as it feels.

  Case example

  > At a disruption meeting, a potential single adopter complained that she had been unsupported. The social workers were horrified and said that they had visited more often than necessary because they knew the placement was at risk. 'That's right', said the carer, 'but you always made me feel you were coming to put your minds at rest, not to support me.'

  Too often, support plans leave it up to the adopters to ask for help, when the assessed needs of the child clearly require ongoing support.

- **A lack of openness in the adoptive family**. Openness in general, rather than open adoption, is the desirable aim; Brodzinsky (2005) compares communicative openness with structural openness.

  Case example

  > Family A declared itself to be in favour of "open adoption" and to welcome direct contact with the birth family. Contact arrangements were meticulously made and adhered to. But each event was hedged in with conditions, limitations and consequently tensions. After a year, the child declined to meet the birth parents and all contact was abruptly terminated.
  >
  > Family B demonstrated an openness in their lifestyle. They accepted that their adopted child had meaningful connections and were prepared to ensure continuity. Indirect letterbox contact became a valued family enterprise and eventually led to regular meetings with the birth family.

- **Not enough preparation of the child or children for the move to permanence.** Children who have settled and made progress in time-limited foster care will not automatically maintain that progress if they have to move again, and they may not be ready to extend their attachments to new carers. Permanence may be a threatening idea for a child, denoting the final severance from birth parents.

  > *The final contact meeting with the birth mother was very emotional – the children clung to her and the mother was equally upset. Eddy ran after the car as his mother was being driven away. There will be letterbox contact but no face-to-face contact. The children are now ready to move on.* (Excerpt from social worker's report read out at a disruption meeting.)

"Final farewells" are rarely advisable. It is not possible for children to internalise a permanent separation from birth parents.

- **Not enough preparation of the prospective carers to parent this particular child or sibling group**. No one can be a parent to any or every child between the age of three and five or to any other category of children. Every child is a singular person and families need the opportunity to "learn the child", however long it takes, after matching, and before introductions.

The last two points regarding preparation really cover all the others. Many previously undiscovered yet significant circumstances can be identified, interpreted and predicted with focused preparation:

- if enough work is put into the period between matching and introduction;
- if a Child Appreciation Day offers a multi-faceted view of the child and the possibility to ask for more;
- if prospective carers and social workers together identify and secure health, education and therapeutic services before placement, and funding is assured before it is required;
- if direct work with the child or children has reached a desired goal;
- if the new family has had ample opportunity to consider how this placement will affect family dynamics;
- if a placement support package, including financial support, has been agreed, and if a continuity plan for the child has been put in place.

It may be, of course, that during this intensive final stage the family will discover that they cannot become the right parents for this child or for this group of children. If they do, it will be less painful for all involved than a disruption later. Every stage of the way to permanence ought to offer the choice of going on or calling a halt. Supporting people to withdraw requires as much skill as enabling them to continue.

COMMON CONCERNS

There are some common concerns about family placement, which also have to be given due consideration:

- the age of the child in relation to other children in the prospective family;
- ethnic, cultural and religious matching;
- placing siblings together or apart: finding families for large sibling groups (sibling placements are further discussed in the next chapter);
- contact needs and prescriptions;

- the child's need to be the only, or by far the youngest, child in the family;
- the difficulties of placing older children, and children with disabilities (disability is further discussed in Chapter 6).

There is enough research evidence (Parker *et al*, 1999) to make us wary of placing children in families that already have a child of similar age. We have all tried to integrate the significance of culture and ethnicity into our practice (Barn, 2000; Prevatt-Goldstein and Spencer, 2000; Thoburn *et al*, 2000; also Adoption Statutory Guidance 2011).

However, a generalised concern for respecting the significance of a child's heritage in matching is insufficient. In assessing a child's needs, social workers should be able to carefully explore and record what they know (and of course what the child knows, if he or she is able to contribute, depending on age and understanding) about his/her identity, ethnicity and culture, and be confident in distinguishing these different concepts (Selwyn *et al*, 2010).

Preserving sibling relationships is an issue central to every aspect of childcare (Neil, 1999; Lord and Borthwick, 2008). We have learned how important it is to keep children in touch with their birth families (Brodzinsky *et al*, 1992; Ryburn, 1994) and we are anxious about establishing contact arrangements in permanent placements (Argent, 2002; Macaskill 2002). If a child has been seriously neglected, we tend to believe he or she will only thrive as an "only" child with the benefit of the new carers' full-time and undivided attention. Experience of featuring children in magazines or websites like *Be My Parent* confirms that it is very hard to find families for older children, large sibling groups and disabled children. If children are seriously disabled, we tend to presume they will need two parents to manage them. All these concerns are real enough and send out warning signals, but we have to beware of making rigid assumptions and writing our guidelines in stone.

- Children have been successfully placed in families that have another child of the same age.
- Some children do well with carers of a different ethnicity in spite of the problems inherent in transracial adoptions.
- Siblings may have to be parted for a variety of reasons but they may also be placed together in amazingly large groups.
- Children and families can negotiate and manage a range of complex contact arrangements.
- The most needy child may do better without being the focus of attention as an only child.
- Young people up to the age of 16, with severe disabilities, have settled in new permanent families, some with single carers.

A new concern is the potential availability of social networking websites to children and families separated by adoption or other permanent placements. Carers need to be prepared to supervise and support their children in the face of these new opportunities and risks.

Every child is unique and every family is unique: good placements cannot be made by ticking boxes and observing rules, but we do need to keep a checklist of known risks very firmly at the back of our minds.

We can try to prevent disruption but we cannot eliminate disruption. We have to find ways to manage and move on from disruption.

5 Sibling groups

SIBLING PLACEMENT DILEMMAS WHEN A DISRUPTION OCCURS

BAAF trainer consultants report that some of the most difficult disruption meetings are those involving sibling placements, when the request has been for the removal of only one child, invariably the oldest. The majority of cases seen by BAAF staff resulted in both or all the children being removed.

In their sample of late permanent placements, Rushton and Dance (2004) reported that, if the new parents requested the removal of one child of a sibling group, prior to the adoption order, the social workers usually decided that either all or none of the group should return to local authority care. However, after the adoption order was granted, there were some cases of one child only leaving the placement.

It isn't only that carers may bond with one child and not another, but one child may refuse to be parented while the other flourishes. One mother quoted by Rushton and Dance (2004) said it all:

> *About two years ago, I think I nearly had a nervous breakdown. I couldn't stop crying and I realised that no matter what I do he will never ever accept me. He tells us, 'you only adopted me because without me you wouldn't have been able to adopt my little brother'.* (p.56)

Case example

Joshua and Rio were brothers aged four-and-a-half and 18 months. They had been together in the same foster placement all Rio's life, and were now being placed for adoption, as their birth family had proved unable to offer them any security or stability. Joshua, in particular, had had to endure very chaotic parenting in his first two years. The foster carers had great difficulty letting the boys go or even collaborating with the adoption plan. On the eve of the move, the foster carers alarmed the adopters with new and fuller information about Joshua's difficulties, which included sexualised behaviour. The boys joined their new family just before Christmas. Support services were due to become available after the holiday. The adopters said

> they had a Christmas of 'hell' with Joshua's behaviour out of control. This continued at his new school in January, with daily calls from teaching staff. Within a few weeks, all agreed that Joshua could not stay, but the adopters and the agency allowed Rio to remain. (From a disruption meeting, 2003)

Faced with the painful task of having to remove one child out of a sibling group, professionals have to assess not only whether these children would do better together or apart, but they will also have to balance the value of a known good placement for one or more against the value of an unknown future for the intact group. Sometimes there is an apprehension that, if the oldest child is "pushed out", the next will follow in due course, but this is not borne out by any of the available studies. What is apparent is that the child, who has already been the most damaged, may be further traumatised by "preferential rejection".

> *Children define themselves by comparing themselves to important others; siblings play a critical role in this definition throughout the life span.* (Groze, 1996)

MAKING SIBLING PLACEMENT DECISIONS

The longer-term implication for risk of disruption, depending on whether siblings are placed 'together or apart' (Lord and Borthwick, 2008), has received some attention. We know that sibling groups are too often separated in the care system and in adoptive placements. Saunders and Selwyn, in their recent study (2011) noted that in 1998–99, a comprehensive analysis of adoptions in 116 local authorities in England (Ivaldi, 2000) had found that 80 per cent of adopted children have birth siblings, but only 37 per cent were placed with siblings. The 37 families who had adopted sibling groups of three or more in Saunders and Selwyn's study reported that 90 per cent of the children were doing well or very well, although many of these families had had to battle with agencies for support and understanding for their task. Nonetheless, as the study concluded, 'adoptive families represent the best chance of securing a better future for the many large sibling groups who are in the care system waiting for a new family'.

One needs to ask: 'who does the child see as siblings?' Not all biologically related children are necessarily close, but on the other hand, children who are not related may validly regard themselves as siblings. Much will depend on shared experiences and individual needs. But it must be remembered that all children have individual needs, yet generally manage to grow up together in their families. Prospective permanent carers need to be open to learning skills that will enable them to support sisters and brothers to live together. Siblings placed together, who have not shared similar experiences in their past, may have different perceptions of their placement. This of course links to the necessity for careful assessment of the needs of each child when planning for sibling groups.

In a survey of children's understanding of their sibling relationships (Edwards *et al*, 2005), it was evident that their relationships with their brothers and sisters are an important part of their everyday lives. A child's feeling that having a sibling means that 'there is always someone there' is significant. Children often talked about older brothers and sisters taking care of and protecting younger siblings, as well as having power over them. Children saw the potential benefit of siblings as a resource.

MINIMISING DISRUPTION RISK IN SIBLING PLACEMENTS

Some experts, such as Groze (1996), in his longitudinal study of special needs adoption, take an emphatic line, now strongly echoed in current guidance, that 'the norm should be that siblings are kept together', and that 'only when there is compelling evidence or when interventions into sibling relations fail should consideration be given to separation'(p.130). He goes on to stress that practitioners need to assess high-risk behaviour, such as sexualised behaviour, sexual offending, and levels of aggression, when placing siblings in a family. We have to assess both the context of this behaviour, and the quality of any attempted intervention. If behaviours are high risk, and the response to appropriate treatment has been minimal, and no family able to cope can be found to take the sibling group, then separation may be necessary as well as inevitable. The need to deal with loss and grief will follow.

Other researchers offer similar advice, if in more qualified terms. Hegar's careful overview of 17 relevant studies (2005) found that:

> *Sibling placements are as stable, or more stable, than placements of single children or separated siblings, and several studies suggest that children do as well or better when placed with their brothers and sisters.* (p.731)

Rushton *et al* (2001) also suggest taking a positive view of sibling placement, while stressing the need always to assess on a case-by-case basis whether particular concerns argue for a different decision (p.153).

However, where placement needs have necessitated sibling separation, Groze (1996) identifies the following tasks:

> *Siblings who are living together prior to being placed apart experience loss and grief related to the separation, regardless of the quality of*

> *the relationship. Siblings need to know why they are being separated, have an opportunity to recognise the change through rituals such as letters, cards or videotapes, and have a clear understanding of what the sibling interactions will be in the future. Siblings who are already placed separately need to know why they will continue to be separated. It is helpful for siblings to meet each other's parent(s) and to know when their next contact will be and how it will occur. It is incumbent upon the adults to plan and facilitate ongoing contact.* (p.130)

THE NEED FOR ASSESSMENT AND SUPPORT

In his research review on siblings, Sanders (2004) noted the high priority that professionals often gave to placing siblings together, but added that this priority:

> *...is not necessarily always reflected either in the placements that ultimately become available for sibling groups or in the emphasis on assessment of sibling relationships. However, where siblings can be placed together, the outcomes tend to be better, but there may be difficulties (sibling rivalry, behavioural difficulties). It can be very difficult for carers taking on a sibling group on a permanent basis. They are likely to need considerable support. (p.197)*

Carers will need to be aware that siblings are likely to recreate or promote patterns in their foster or adoptive homes that replicate their experiences in their birth families, entailing problematic interactions and behaviour patterns.

Case example

> Ruby, aged seven, was placed in permanent foster care with her two younger brothers. She had been left to look after them by her birth mother when they lived at home and now resented the foster carer "taking over". The placement of all three children nearly disrupted, but a play therapist was able to help Ruby and the carer to "share" parenting the little boys. This allowed Ruby to let go of her feelings of responsibility more gradually; it provided continuity for the younger children and formed an alliance between Ruby and the carer.

We should take care when assessing a child as "parentified". It may be a valid description or a Eurocentric assumption; in other cultures it could be the norm for older children to care for their younger brothers and sisters.

In their study, Rushton *et al* (2001) found that specialist help with sibling relationships was rare; direct work tended to focus on parents and children separately. The authors noted:

> *There is currently little guidance or training available to social workers needing to help children in their relationships with brothers and sisters and it is clear that this is a crucial area of practice...Post-placement services must include sibling therapy as the children and families work out their new and evolving relationship.* (p.156)

Although the complexity of children's understanding of their relationships with their siblings, and the shifts these relationships undergo over time, make it hard to extrapolate hard and fast practice rules regarding placement stability, the emerging research provides some important guidance towards making good assessments in each unique case. An awareness of the dynamics of sibling placements, together or apart, is an essential ingredient when dealing with disruption.

Useful assessment tools include:

- *The Sibling Relationship Checklists* (Department of Health 1991, reproduced as an appendix in Lord and Borthwick, 2008)
- *The Framework for the Assessment of Children in Need and Their Families* (Department of Health *et al*, 2000)
- *Ten Top Tips for Placing Siblings* (Argent, 2008)

6

Disabled children

It is bad enough when a placement disrupts, for whatever reason; if the child has a disability, everyone will feel even worse about it. The birth parents may be confirmed in their fear that they have produced an "unacceptable" child; social workers can become immobilised by the fear that further work could do further harm; prospective carers, who, despite their best efforts, could not fulfil a promise or sustain a commitment, may fear that they have only guilt to contribute to any future plan. If they themselves are disabled, they may also fear that that their disability will be blamed. And children will almost certainly fear that their impairment caused the disruption. Tanya, aged six, said, 'I had too many fits' when her placement ended.

Because it is difficult to find placements for disabled children, there is a danger that, after disruption, disabled children could remain in the wrong place for the wrong reason for a long time. If a carefully chosen placement does not work out, it is easy to become disheartened about finding another. Perhaps a reassessment of needs is required; if a placement disrupts, could something have occurred that has more to do with the child's care history than their disability?

Case example

Denise moved to a well-prepared family from a residential home for children with disabilities – where she had lived almost since birth – when she was nine years old. The family expected the withdrawn behaviour, the epileptic fits, the learning difficulties and the speech impairment. They had gathered all they could about Denise's disabilities from the agency medical adviser and the local paediatrician; they had spent hours with her residential workers and her teachers. They had an older disabled daughter by birth and belonged to a network of parents who also had children with disabilities. They were committed to Denise and were certain that she would become a permanent member of their family.

Unfortunately, no-one had warned them about Denise's habit of wandering around the house, emptying out every drawer and cupboard she could find and then carefully putting back the contents in the wrong places. This behaviour had apparently not disturbed anyone in the residential home, where children had few personal

> belongings and where access to kitchen, bathrooms and staff rooms was guarded; it was even seen as something that gave Denise hours of harmless enjoyment and left the staff free to cope with more troublesome children.
>
> For the new family it was the worst scenario. The mother spent all day looking for cutlery among her underwear and rescuing documents from the linen cupboard. The father, who worked from home, had to lock away every piece of paper and office equipment. The older daughter became upset because all her toys and clothes were messed up.
>
> The more the family tried to distract Denise from her obsessive occupation, the more determined and secretive she became about her business. After one particularly trying day, when the carers thought they had finally managed to persuade Denise to restrict herself to her own cupboards, she got up in the middle of the night to do her dreadful deeds!

The unforeseen circumstance in this placement was not only Denise's quirky behaviour, but also the family's need for order. The parents had made tremendous emotional and psychological adjustments when their disabled daughter was born and they went on making adjustments. They rightly regarded themselves as a flexible couple. But they had a sticking point: they had to keep control of the material things in life to counterbalance that flexibility. They could no more have verbalised this need, or foreseen its relevance to Denise's placement, than the residential workers could visualise the shattering effect of what they regarded as Denise's unremarkable habit on the family.

The placement disrupted after six weeks. Denise did not fully understand why she had to go back to the children's home. Her preoccupation with drawers faded when a play therapist opened up the recesses of Denise's life story – work that had previously been attempted but abandoned. The staff backed up the therapy with a behaviour modification programme, so that the habit as well as the obsession were tackled. It was a slow process, with several setbacks, but a year later Denise was successfully placed with a family. (Denise's story is quoted in Argent and Kerrane, 1997.)

Some disabled children, unlike Denise, are very aware of the social model of disability, which takes into account the role that society plays in disabling a person with an impairment. George said to his social worker, who collected him when his placement disrupted, 'they called me a wheelchair child and spent all their time fussing about the doors and the ramps – but I'm a boy who uses a wheelchair and they didn't know the difference'. Children can become disabled by an over-emphasis on their impairments. Or it may be that the disability obscures the child.

Case example

> A couple in their early thirties had a birth son with Down's syndrome and five years later successfully adopted a three-year-old boy with Down's syndrome. They then applied to adopt a girl, aged two, also with Down's syndrome. The placement disrupted after six months because neither of the parents could "take" to this child. The preparation had been all about the stresses of caring for three children with the same disability but the history and personality of the little girl had been quite overlooked.

It is, of course, important to prepare families for dealing with impairment. George's prospective adopters were used to a wheelchair, but every wheelchair is different; an electric wheelchair can become quite overwhelming in a regular-sized house, and experience of one wheelchair need not be a blueprint for living with another. A parent who adopted a girl with cerebral palsy said: 'next time place the wheelchair first and the child later'.

In her longitudal study of 123 adopters caring for disabled children, Laraine Glidden (2006) found that families who adopt children with, or at risk of, developmental delay, adjust quickly to their parenting roles, and report positive outcomes soon after the placement as well as 5, 11, and 17 years later. As a group, they remain non-depressed, report high marital satisfaction, low levels of family disharmony, and subjective well-being. They continue to remain involved with their children as the children approach the transition to adulthood, and report many rewards as they anticipate their adult children's future life in areas of work, socialisation and family. Most of these families also had biological, step, other adopted or long-term fostered children; 27 per cent of the families were already living with the child on a fostering basis when they made the decision to adopt. Some families were quite large and had adopted more than one child with disabilities; 44 per cent of the sample had five or more children, and the parents in the large families were functioning as well as or better than parents in the smaller families.

It is not surprising that disruptions happen when children, carers, and social workers have to mix and try to match their experiences, attitudes and expectations of disability with other complex matters such as attachment patterns and models of child care, family systems, rights and responsibilities, contact and continuity, and ethnicity, culture and religion. It can cost three times as much to bring up a child with an impairment than a child without disabilities; the stresses of fighting for all the services a disabled child may need can wear out the most energetic parents; the emotional weight of caring for a disabled child can become overwhelming. It is remarkable and a tribute to all concerned that the disruption rate for children with impairments is lower than for children who are not disabled (Cousins, 2006). And the disability itself is only rarely the cause of the disruption.

7
A cry for help or a plea for closure?

When is a disruption not a disruption? If Cheryl, a 16-year-old who was placed aged 11, explodes out of her foster home during a particularly turbulent adolescence, and the distraught carers turn to social services for help, has the placement disrupted? Or has it reached a critical stage in a life-long process? If Aaron's parents find that they can no longer cope with the severely disabled child they adopted as a baby 14 years ago, and request a residential placement, is that the end of the adoption or the beginning of a new phase?

Much will depend on the attitude of social services and on the resilience of the carers.

CASE EXAMPLES

> Cheryl left her permanent foster family's home on her 16th birthday, in anger. She was accommodated by social services. For a year she refused to see her foster carers or to speak to them on the telephone, but she sent them abusive little notes in reply to their regular calm letters with family news. When Cheryl was 17, she was given her own flat; she asked her foster mother to help her with the curtains. Two years later, her foster father proudly gave her away at her wedding.

Cheryl's social worker always included the foster carers in planning for Cheryl, and the carers never faltered in regarding Cheryl as one of the family. Disruption did not become an issue.

In contrast, Aaron's social worker was punitive towards the adoptive parents because she considered that they had failed him.

> The local authority applied for a care order on the grounds that Aaron, aged 15, was at risk because his adoptive parents were emotionally and physically no longer able to cope with his impairments. The adopters wanted to retain sole responsibility for Aaron but they felt too guilty to oppose the order. Aaron was placed in a residential home at a great distance from his family. Contact was not supported and

social services did not hesitate to call it a disruption. The adopters visited whenever they could until Aaron died, aged 19.

There is often a very fine line between a desperate cry for help and a plea for closure. The symptoms and messages may be almost identical. Families under pressure will ask for more of everything and anything in an attempt to make it come out right. Complaints will become more vociferous and will be levelled at an increasing number of organisations and individuals. The carers will become more despondent, the children more disturbing, and the social workers more anxious. The diagram opposite gives an idea of the similarities and the differences between needing help either to carry on or to let go. It can provide a useful tool to explore together with the carers which point they have reached.

INTERVENTION MEETINGS

A cry for help by carers who have nearly, but not quite, reached their limits, may be well answered by an "intervention meeting". It is important to stress at the very beginning that this meeting is to enhance the placement, not to unpick it. Its purpose is:

- to demonstrate support for the carers and the child;
- to move on and not get stuck;
- to share and acknowledge feelings rather than apportion blame;
- to identify issues leading to placement difficulties;
- to agree the child's and the carers' current needs;
- to make plans to provide for needs or to state clearly if and why any needs cannot be met;
- to set time limits for action and dates to monitor progress;
- to hear and understand the child's wishes and feelings;
- to leave the door open for continuation or disruption.

Figure 1: A cry for help or a plea for closure?

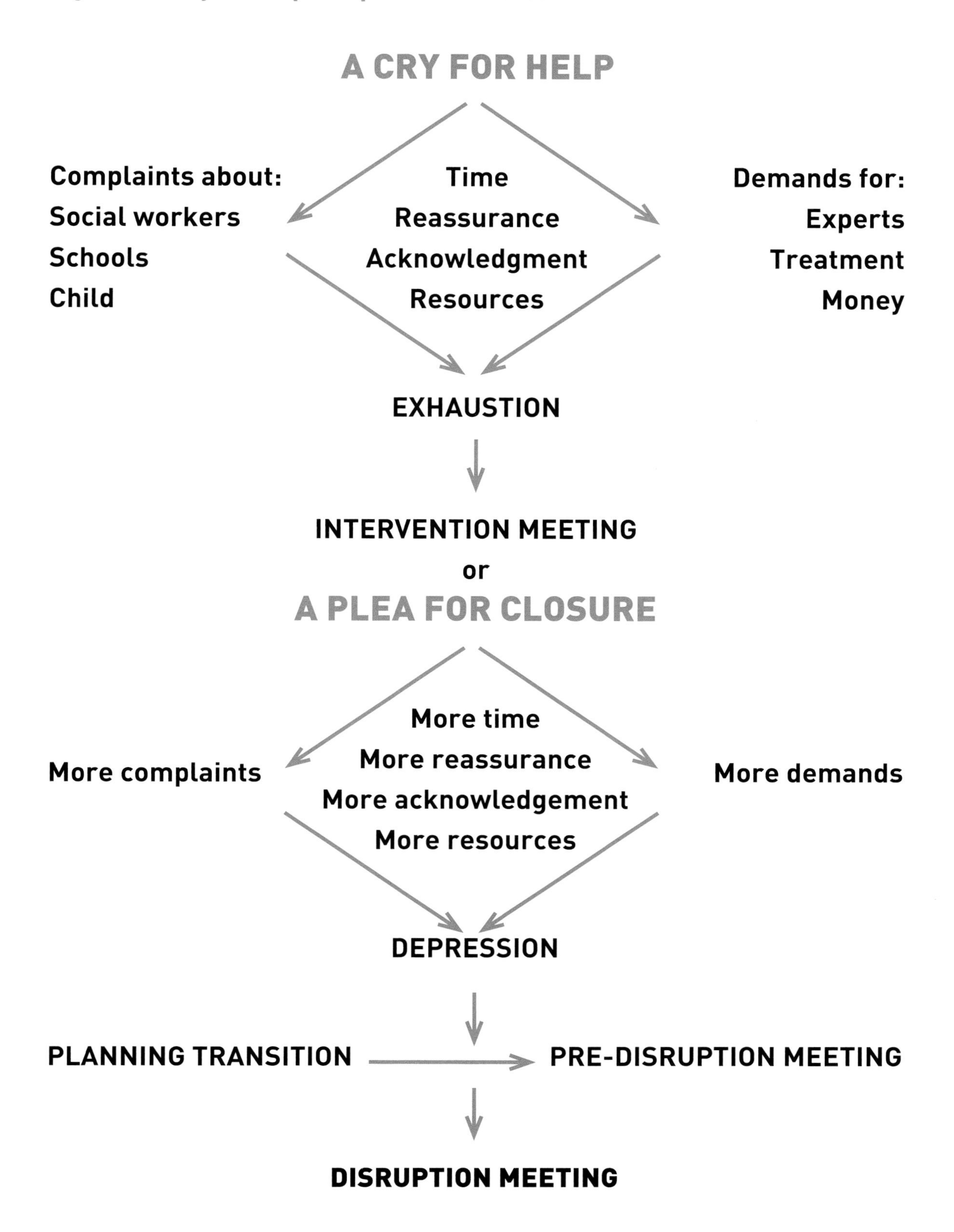

The agenda will depend on the presenting situation and should be carer-led with the support of an independent Chair. It may include specific items to do with health and education or therapy, parenting skills, short breaks, continuity issues, access to information and unmet expectations. Who should attend will need to be agreed with the carers. Direct or indirect involvement of the child should always be considered a possibility while taking into account the child's age and understanding. The carers may choose to include relatives and friends, to invite professionals of their choice, previous carers, or even their lawyer if there is a legal problem.

It is essential that all the social workers concerned attend together with managers empowered to make decisions. Agencies will follow their own guidelines for allocating scarce resources, but there is nothing more frustrating at crisis point than to be told, for instance, that it will take someone "so and so" long to decide whether an identified need can be funded. In order to ensure that real progress can be made during the meeting, the Chair will want to brief the social work team about the agenda beforehand. It is important to record all decisions so that there can be no doubt about what action will be taken as a result of the meeting.

An intervention meeting is not like a routine review and should not be a substitute for other scheduled meetings. It has to have an element of "specialness" in order to validate the carers' concerns and perhaps distress. It is most like a "Child Appreciation Day", only now the carers are the experts with the most immediate experience of the child. It is not set up to comply with regulations but to ask the questions: What helps? What doesn't? And what would help more? Enough time, preferably a whole day, nurturing refreshments, a welcoming venue, videos, photographs and other visual aids will give positive messages.

Example

The carers are overwhelmed by what they see as the child's rejecting and destructive behaviour. Divide a flip chart into three columns. In column 1 ask the carers (and relatives or friends if present) to list what the child does. In column 2 ask them to list how each behaviour makes them feel. Then in column 3 ask the carers and others to list how they think the child might be feeling. Invite discussion about how changing the response might change the behaviour.

The last item on the agenda should allow the carers and the child to trust that they will be supported whatever the outcome, and that even disruption is not the end of the story.

PREPARING FOR DISRUPTION

It could be said that planning disruptions should be as painstaking a task as planning introductions. For the child both are life-changing transitions, which most of us never have to endure. If prospective carers finally have to give up, it does not mean that they have become uncaring; they are still the same people who impressed social workers, panel members and referees enough to have the child placed with them.

Unless there is an unexpected risk to the child, the prospective permanent carers should be as involved in the move away as they were when the child came to them. The child's needs have to be the focus.

- Who will say what, when and where to the child?
- How gradual or abrupt will the actual move be?
- Who will take or collect the child (two people are needed for car journeys, one to drive and one to concentrate on the child)?
- How will clothes and other belongings be transferred?
- How will continuity for the child be maintained?

If there has been an intervention support meeting before the disruption, the carers are less likely to demand an instant ending or to abandon the child at the agency's offices in a final act of desperation. If the carers do not opt out of the process, the child will feel more valued and may begin to see the disruption as part of a continuing story.

8

Disruption meetings

Disruption meetings are generally associated with adoption breakdown, but are equally applicable to permanent fostering arrangements.

PURPOSE

The purpose of a disruption meeting is:

- to enable participants to share information and feelings about the adoption process, the placement and the disruption without assigning blame;
- to facilitate increased understanding of everyone's actions and points of view;
- to explore all the factors that may have contributed to disruption;
- to explore and identify the current needs of the child, the carers, the birth family and the agency or agencies;
- to formulate future plans for the child based on what has been learned from the disruption;
- to highlight areas for development in policy and practice.

THE DISRUPTION MEETING

When?

Everyone needs time to recover from a disruption before they can reflect on what happened, but they also need to retain a clear memory of events. To hold a meeting before people are ready may be counter-productive; to postpone a meeting for too long risks people getting into defended and entrenched positions. About five to ten weeks after disruption seems to work well, but there can be no rules about timing. The important thing is to enable children and families to regard disruption meetings as an integral part of placement support.

How long?

Disruption meetings usually take the whole day. It is vital for everyone to be able to say what should be said, to know that they have been heard, and to listen to everyone else. There has to be time to digress, to reconsider, to recall, and to be upset. Each person has to feel that they can make a contribution to the child's future.

Where?

A warm, light, well-ventilated room with comfortable chairs, informally arranged, will generally give a reassuring message. It is almost impossible to hold a successful disruption meeting around a conference table. We have been told that some workers and families would feel threatened without a large table to protect them, but the preparation for disruption meetings should allay all fears of attack. It is preferable not to meet in local authority offices. Hot and cold drinks and biscuits should be available throughout the day; a sandwich lunch in the meeting room will help to keep the momentum going. A tactfully placed box of tissues is advisable.

Who?

Who will speak for the child? And if the child and/or the carers are from a minority ethnic group, where will the cultural competence come from?

Everyone who has been involved before, during and after the placement could have valuable observations to make. Previous and current carers as well as the permanent or prospective permanent carers, perhaps members of the birth family, teachers, therapists, medical advisers, psychologists, possibly police officers, health visitors, GPs and, of course, assorted social workers and a panel representative could contribute; most well-attended meetings will have between 12 and 20 participants. If anyone wishes to bring a friend or outside support worker, they should generally be enabled to do so, but if child protection concerns are in conflict with openness, the Chair should always adopt the safest course. It can be very enlightening to have the views of the carers' grown-up or teenage children; they can often say what their parents find too difficult to tell.

It may be that carers want to bring their solicitor, especially if there is acrimony, or if the placement has been terminated by the local authority against their wishes. It is unproductive to get into adversarial positions at a disruption meeting and the carers should be helped to feel confident that a lawyer will not be needed. However, if they insist on having their solicitor, the local authority legal department should be consulted and may wish to send a representative. A decision has to be made about what would be constructive for a particular disruption meeting and what would not. But constructive must not be construed as uncritical.

If it is absolutely impossible for potential contributors to attend the meeting, then it is absolutely necessary for their views to be presented by a designated person, either orally or in a report.

INVOLVING THE CHILD

Young people who are the subjects of disruption meetings should be encouraged to talk to their social worker and the convenor of the meeting about how they can be involved. If children are to participate in the meeting, they need careful preparation. They will have to be fully aware of their own history as well as the purpose and aims of disruption meetings. They should know who will be there and what will be discussed; they should have a preview of the layout and the room where the meeting will be held, and they should have an informal chat with the Chair before they go in to the meeting. Sometimes it is necessary for the Chair to visit the child ahead of the disruption meeting to help ascertain their views, and to assess how, and whether, the child should attend. Depending on age, understanding, and the particular circumstances, it may be preferable to organise the agenda so that the child attends for only part of the day. If geography and timing allow, it might be possible to invite the child to join the meeting after school or during the lunch break. If children are too young, too distressed, or too fragile to be directly involved, it may still be important for them to know who will tell their story and how it will be presented. Or they may want to write a letter to be read at the meeting. If they do, a reply from the Chair after the meeting would be welcome.

> Dear meeting
>
> I am very sorry I cant live with Sue and Gery. I want to have a famly but I want to stay in my foster home. I dont want to go to a diferent town. I like Sue and Gerry but I cant be good for them. I cant help it I was reelly bad for them. I hurt the dog. I sceamed in the nite. I just want to screem if I have to move again. I miss Sue and Gery lots and I want to keep seeing my Mum and big brother and I wish I cud see my Dad.

> Dear Leslie,
>
> Thank you for your letter to the disruption meeting. It was very helpful to have your description of what happened and for everyone to know how you felt about leaving Sue and Gerry. They miss you too, and Diane, your new social worker, is going to make sure that you can keep in touch.
>
> We were pleased to hear that you feel settled, back with your foster carer in your own home town; we hope it will be possible for you to stay with her and to see your Mum and brother regularly. I'm afraid no one has managed to find your Dad so far, but they will keep on trying.
>
> Perhaps you would like to know what everyone else said at the meeting. Diane will talk to you about it next time she visits. She will also bring back your life story book so that you can do some more work on it together. We wondered whether you would like her to help you write a letter to your old social worker to tell her where you are now; she would be so pleased to hear from you.
>
> We were all thinking of you during the meeting and wish you a Happy Birthday for next Saturday.

With sensitive support, disruption meetings can help some young people to see their situation more clearly and to believe that everyone tried and still cares.

If the child or children do not attend, it can be inspiring to create a symbolic presence. A large photograph placed somewhere in the middle of the room, perhaps on an empty chair, can work wonders to concentrate the mind.

MANAGING DISRUPTION MEETINGS

Convening disruption meetings is a daunting task. It is a meeting no one anticipates with pleasure. Families who are still struggling with conflicting feelings do not find it easy to attend although they may be clamouring to be heard. Social workers could be reluctant to share critical opinions or to have their practice scrutinised. Former carers and birth family members often feel resentful and angry. Teachers and therapists may consider themselves to be outside the adoption process. And the child, even if old and resilient enough, may prefer to stay away.

The convenor has to take responsibility for the preparation, co-ordination and liaison necessary to stage effective disruption meetings. It is common practice for the child's social worker to be the convenor, but agencies may like to consider whether it would be better for one designated person in the department to develop expertise in this sensitive area of work. Some outside agencies may offer a complete disruption service, including an independent Chair, a convenor and a minute taker.

The convenor's tasks

- To be available for advice and guidance about the proposed meeting
- To appoint an independent Chair and arrange for relevant papers to be sent
- To consult with the Chair and the social workers involved about who should be invited and, specifically, whether and how to include the child
- To make sure that all parties are invited and consulted about dates, travel and childcare arrangements, and have the support they require in order to participate in a disruption meeting (see Appendix 2)
- To follow-up the initial approach with written information about the purpose and aims of disruption meetings in general (see Appendix 3)
- To find and book a suitable venue
- To agree an agenda for the meeting with the Chair
- To send out formal invitations together with the agenda: people will feel more comfortable if they know what to expect; they should be offered an opportunity for further discussion before the meeting (see Appendix 2)
- To organise catering arrangements
- To appoint a minute taker and circulate the minutes when they have been agreed by the Chair
- To circulate the Chair's report (see Appendix 6)
- To organise follow-up meetings within the department in order to discuss the Chair's report and monitor action resulting from the meeting and the report.

This list may sound daunting, but all the tasks are commonsensical steps on the way to making the best of disruption. Each step takes time and sufficient time should be allocated. There will only be one disruption meeting, and it's as well to put in the resources to make it a good one.

9
Chairing disruption meetings

Chairs of disruption meetings should not have line management responsibility for the child's or the carers' social workers. If it is an inter-agency placement, they should be independent of both agencies. Where agencies belong to a consortium, they may well provide Chairs for each other's disruption meetings, but there is then a danger of familiarity and sympathy with shared problems. The same goes for Independent Reviewing Officers who work for one of the agencies involved in a disruption. As well as being independent, the Chair should be experienced in adoption and fostering, used to dealing with large meetings in informal settings, and be able to write a comprehensive readable report. The ethnicity of the Chair may be significant if the meeting concerns children and/or families from minority ethnic groups.

No one involved in adoption can entirely detach themselves from its dynamics, and a disruption meeting Chair cannot remain entirely unaffected by the dominant myths in which adoption policy is clothed.

> *...they (adoption professionals) are bound by the same narratives and myths, subject to the same emotional need to rescue and to blame, and buffeted by the same powerful media and political forces as the other points in the triangle...* (Treacher and Katz, 2000, p.216)

Chairpersons will have their own way of dealing with disruption meetings, but it is always vital to work closely with the convenor and to be aware of agency policy and practice. Some Chairs want to know only basic facts about a case before the meeting; others will request more detailed information, which may include some or all of the following:

- the child's Form E with history of child and birth family (for adoption in Scotland or for foster care in the UK) and/or Child's Permanence Report/ Child's Adption Assessment Report (in England and Wales);
- the carer's Form F or Prospective Adopter's Report;
- the Adoption Placement Report (or foster care agreement) and record of agency follow-up if relevant;
- minutes from linking and/or matching panels;
- outline of the Adoption Placement Plan, which should include the introduction plan;
- placement support plan including contact arrangements;

- placement records including reviews;
- inter-agency agreements (usually Forms H1 and H2);
- summary of events prior to disruption and present situation.

If the disruption has given rise to a complaint or to child safeguarding concerns, the Chair needs to achieve a balance between seeing and sharing information relevant to the disruption and not compromising any other formal agency process.

The court has to give leave if it is advisable for the Chair to see the Children's Guardian's report (England and Wales) or any other court papers. Court reports in Scottish proceedings would not normally be used. The court would have to be asked for permission to open the process and copy any papers sought.

THE AGENDA

It is best if the Chair, having had the agreed information, can devise an agenda to circulate before the meeting. Most people are apprehensive about coming to disruption meetings; if carers can go through the agenda with their support workers, they usually feel better prepared to contribute. A useful agenda for a disruption meeting might include some, or even all, of the following:

Introductions and purpose of meeting

- **The child's life in the birth family**
  Attachment patterns and behaviour
  Quality of parental care
  Physical, emotional and intellectual health and development
  Changes and moves, losses and continuity
  Nurseries and schools
  Role in the family, sibling relations
- **The child's history in care**
  Placements and moves
  Relationships and recovery
  Coping mechanisms and behaviour
  Continuity and contact
  Education, health and development
  Preparation for move to permanence
  The child's voice
- **The permanent family's progress from application to matching**
  Information and communication
  Assessment, training, general preparation

Preparation to meet specific child's needs
Awareness of separation and continuity issues
The carers' other children, relatives and support network
Apprehensions and expectations

- **Agency practice**
  Permanency plan
  Recruitment, matching decision, permanency panel's recommendations
  Contact arrangements
  Inter-departmental and inter-agency liaison
  How is information shared between agencies?
  Direct work with child
  Post-placement support services
  Compliance with statutory and practice guidance

- **The birth family's involvement**
  Attitude to local authority's intervention and to working together and with social workers
  Understanding of child's needs
  View of foster care and adoption
  Contribution to continuity for child
  The child's voice

- **The introduction**
  How was plan negotiated?
  Was there a Child Appreciation Day?
  Did carers meet birth relatives, current and previous carers and medical advisers/therapists?
  Timing, liaison, monitoring, review and feedback
  Arrangements for continuity
  Hopes and warnings
  The child's voice

- **The placement**
  Family systems, lifestyles and relationships
  Ethnicity, culture and religion
  Progress and regression, rewards and challenges
  Home and school, health and stress
  The carers' other children
  Contact and continuity
  Formal and informal supports and services
  Adjustments and sticking points
  The child's voice

- **The disruption**
  Process leading to disruption, decision to end placement
  Preparation for disruption, child's perception of disruption
  Impact of disruption on child and family members

Management of disruption
Plans for continuity, support after disruption

- **The present and the future**
  The child's current placement, implications for stability and permanence, legal status
  The child's wishes
  Further assessments, treatment plans and direct work
  Continuity and contact arrangements with birth family and carers
  Education and health
  The carer's situation
  Rights and responsibilities
  Future childcare plans and support needs
  The birth family's circumstances
  Involvement in future plans for the child
  Changes in the family, particularly with reference to siblings
  The agency's position
  Responsibilities, inter-agency liaison
  Lessons for practice, messages for policy
  Plans for action and review
- **Summing up and recommendations**

VISUAL AIDS

Visual aids will allow participants to share a starting point for the meeting, and to focus on the child. Two flipcharts, which can be prepared before the meeting, are enough. Anything more technical is inclined to dilute attention.

Example

On one chart, make a flow diagram of all the child's transitions, including changes in the birth family home, change of nurseries and schools, and moves within the care system. On the other chart, make a representational drawing of the child's losses: for instance, a child holding three balloons, one with birth family losses, one with lost carers, social workers and teachers, and one with material losses, such as houses, toys and schools. As people arrive for the meeting, the Chair can introduce them to the diagrams, while they enjoy refreshments.

Case example

Jay, now aged six, was said to have had a stable home life and few moves in care before she was placed for adoption. The flow chart showed that Jay had moved house six times with her mother before she was removed from home, aged four, on an Emergency Protection Order. During this time, her mother had three different partners, and on two occasions abandoned Jay with her maternal grandmother, who was an invalid. Jay lived in two different foster homes, with regular short break placements, while a permanent family was recruited. She changed nurseries and schools six times. Her losses filled the three balloons (see Appendices 4 and 5).

Other visual aids can be devised to suit other situations. Family trees and family circles could illustrate the child's and the carers' stories. Or, if nothing springs to mind as appropriate, messages of welcome and reassuring statements may be written large in coloured pens.

Example

On Flipchart 1

Disruption is rarely the result of what one party has done or left undone. It is usually a combination of:

UNIDENTIFIED CIRCUMSTANCES

MISINTERPRETED CIRCUMSTANCES

UNPREDICTABLE CIRCUMSTANCES

On Flipchart 2

NO ONE IS TO BLAME FOR THE DISRUPTION

EVERYONE HAS FEELINGS ABOUT THE DISRUPTION

THERE IS MORE THAN ONE WAY OF VIEWING THE DISRUPTION

THE INTRODUCTIONS

- It is always important for the Chair to acknowledge, at the beginning of the meeting, that this is a distressing occasion for all concerned but that the aim is for positive outcomes. Usually everyone present has had high hopes of this placement, which makes it even harder for them now, and they may have to be reminded that the carers are still the competent people who were thought to be the right parents for this child, or these children.
- It is a good idea to repeat the purpose of all disruption meetings, and to establish an anti-racist/sexist/disablist/ageist framework from the word go.
- People need time to introduce themselves; later they may need time to go outside to have a breath of fresh air or to have a weep and recover or

just to have a comfort break, and they should know that time, as well as refreshments, are readily available.

- While it is preferable for everyone to stay for the whole day, it may not always be possible; if people have to come and go, they should be appreciated for doing their best.
- An explanation should be given about the purpose of minutes and reports; agreement should be reached about who will receive them and when that will be. (This is discussed in more detail in Chapter 13.)

WORKING THROUGH THE AGENDA

- Working through the agenda will take the best part of the day. Some Chairs take their own notes, others rely on the minutes. Some items will take a long time to discuss, others will be dealt with briefly.
- The person with the most relevant information or feelings about each section should be asked to speak first, but everyone should have the opportunity to contribute at every stage.
- Participants should be given time to refer to notes and to consult with each other if appropriate. Social workers should be asked to bring all relevant documents including files, however heavy. Retrieving a piece of buried information may prove invaluable to fill a gap in the narrative.
- The Chair has to enable everyone to feel safe enough to voice difficult feelings.
- It is best to have a short, informal lunch break with sandwiches brought into the meeting room. This encourages the group to go on talking together and helps to avoid conflicts and alliances. It also helps to prevent the "after lunch doldrums".
- It is important both to cover everything on the agreed agenda and to finish on time. Otherwise people may have to leave without taking positive messages from the meeting.

THE SUMMING UP

- Themes: the recurring concerns of the day have to be drawn together, e.g. continuity, stability, preparation, attachment, openness, support.
- Vulnerabilities: carers should not feel that they have failed, workers should not feel they got it all wrong and, above all, the child should feel

positive about future plans. If mistakes have been made, it is because we all make mistakes.

- Tensions: difficult relationships between adopters, foster carers and agencies or between departments or agencies have to be reviewed and acknowledged.
- Recommendations: the meeting should have an opportunity to discuss what has been learned from this disruption and how this might affect policy and practice, e.g. school and health transfers, Child Appreciation Days, assessments, sharing information, inter-agency procedures.

Case examples

> The disruption meeting for Arleen, aged ten, was attended by her prospective adopters, previous and present foster carers, birth mother, teacher and social workers from both the child's and the adopters' agencies. There had been contact with birth parents and foster carers and intensive social work support throughout the six-month turbulent placement. The meeting was planned before Arleen left the adopters but after she had almost set their house on fire. It took place a month after she had returned to her previous foster home in order to give everyone time to begin to recover and look towards the future. Arleen joined the meeting when she came home from school. She listened to a summary of what had been said and added her version of the story. Arleen remained with her foster carers. She had already moved 27 times and it seemed she could not invest in permanence away from the birth family but she could manage in a safe and stable foster home where she was not expected to make a total commitment. The prospective parents went on to adopt a sister and brother aged eight and ten.

Brad's disruption meeting was very different. The prospective adopters had been hailed as a perfect match and their cries for help remained unheard until it was too late.

> This was an inter-agency placement where each agency blamed the other for the problems leading up to the disruption. Information had not been freely exchanged and some vital information had been unintentionally withheld from the adopters. Brad, aged five, had said a "final goodbye" to his mother two weeks before placement and there were no plans for future face-to-face contact. Adoption support was limited to specific requests, which became irritatingly frequent for social workers. The family had been promised therapeutic help but after five months they were still waiting. By this time, Brad had completely rejected his adoptive mother and was making sexual overtures to strangers. No one discussed the possibility of disruption with this seemingly perfect couple. They abandoned Brad abruptly in their local social services office when they could bear no more.

> Six months later, the child's agency called a disruption meeting because Brad had not settled in his foster home and would have to move again. The adopters refused to come to the meeting or to send any comments – they would not even speak to the social worker on the telephone. The adopters' agency did not send anyone because they were some distance away and could not spare the time. The birth mother had apparently disappeared. Brad's new social worker came to the meeting but did not know the history, and her line manager, who did, was called away in the middle of the meeting. A family placement worker, who had not been involved, attended the meeting and was ready to step in if asked to find another permanent family. The foster care support worker came with the current carers. This turned into a departmental planning meeting with an independent Chair but without enough information about the disruption to make informed decisions. (Quoted in Argent, 2003)

It needs to be acknowledged that a meeting fully attended, with the active involvement of the key participants, which successfully focuses on the task, will not necessarily be a comfortable meeting to chair.

10

Alternative models

There is more than one way of looking back on disruption, learning from the process, and moving on. The format described in the previous chapter will not suit every situation. If child safeguarding issues have been raised, more consideration will have to be given to matters of confidentiality. Who knows, and who needs to know, the facts? And how will a disruption meeting fit in with other necessary forms of inquiry? If the adopters are too bruised or angry to attend a meeting, can another formula be found to include their views and to share outcomes with them? It may be that a full hearing of their side of the story, before a disruption meeting, will enable them to contribute to the broader view. If inter-agency, or inter-departmental disagreements threaten to prevent constructive discussion, the professionals may have to do some sorting out on their own before they can look ahead.

Whichever model is used, it should preserve the essence of disruption meetings: an independent exploration of frequently conflicting and previously unexpressed views, which can lead to a better and richer understanding for all concerned, and open the way for healing and for moving on.

SHORT MEETINGS

Half-day meetings along the same lines as a full day are perhaps the least satisfactory. It will not be possible to create a rounded picture of events or to make considered plans for the future if the Chair has to set tight time limits for each item, or if sections have to be omitted, or potential contributors are not invited. Rushing through an agenda can leave some participants with re-awakened but unresolved feelings. Whether a short meeting will be better than no meeting will depend on the circumstances.

HOME-BASED MEETINGS

Occasionally, if they request it, disruption meetings can be held in the prospective carers' home. It may be the only way the carers, and perhaps the child, can attend or feel secure enough to contribute. It is one way of validating their significance. The convenor will have to work closely with the family and the Chair to make suitable arrangements. Where can people go if they feel upset or need a break? What will happen if children come home from school, if the telephone rings or if the neighbour calls? Refreshments should be provided by the agency or, if the family wants to be in charge of hospitality, a large cake to finish off the afternoon will usually not go amiss.

SPLIT DAY MEETINGS

If families feel unable to join a meeting but want to contribute in person, it may be appropriate for the Chair to visit them at home in the morning, preferably with a minute taker and their support worker, before holding a full scale meeting in the afternoon. In this case the Chair would take responsibility for feeding in the carers' views at each relevant point during the second half of the meeting, which could then be office-based. If distances are too great, the two sessions may have to be held on different days.

ONE-TO-ONE

It is possible to explore the causes of a disruption in order to plan for the future without holding any kind of conventional meeting. An independent Chair can be appointed to interview all the parties, including the child. If, for instance, the carers or an agency are making a formal complaint, this may be the only feasible process, but it should not be confused with an inquiry into who is to blame for what; it should still be focused on the purpose of disruption meetings. The Chair must then draw the threads together and present a detailed report with recommendations that will reflect a composite view.

PAPER ASSESSMENTS

If all else fails, an independent person, experienced in disruption, can be asked to examine all available documentation and to make comments and recommendations accordingly. This is clearly not a "best buy", but it is better than losing the history and the experience of disruption altogether. The resulting report can be circulated to all the parties and may be received as evidence of respect for the past and some hope for the future.

KINSHIP PLACEMENTS

Disruption has particularly complex connotations for kinship carers because there has already been at least one family crisis, and now here they are, actively involved in another. It is easy to overlook the needs of kinship carers because they themselves may feel that they have failed and have no right to further support; they may want to distance themselves from authority and choose to stay away from a disruption meeting. But the impact of the disruption will reverberate through the whole family and kinship carers frequently have to cope not only with their own feelings, conflicting loyalties and depression, but they also become targets of their relatives' anger and resentment. A Family Group Conference may be more appropriate than a disruption meeting when kinship placements have to end.

FOLLOW-UP

In some circumstances, it could be helpful and advisable for the Chair to meet or speak on the telephone with the parties individually before a formal disruption meeting.

It should go without saying that the value of examining disruptions has to be measured by what follows. Have new plans for the child led to stability? Have the carers been able to move on from their distress? Have social workers had the necessary support to change practice? Have social work managers taken on board implications for policy? Professional follow-up reviews are essential if disruption meetings are to be more than one-off events to bury a placement.

11

Continuity after disruption

Children and young people who have to be separated from their birth families nearly always lose some of the threads of their life stories; the continuity of their lives is shattered by a series of complex and unusual transitions. Being removed from home to live with strangers, and moving from one set of strangers to another, are surely two of the most traumatic changes any child can face. And the majority of children in care have to face them more than once. Every time they move, another set of memories is lost or distorted because, with the best intentions, life cannot be wholly recorded in a book. When permanent placements disrupt, the threat to continuity increases because preserving continuity is not uppermost in most people's minds during times of stress. There is also a danger of professionals taking a punitive attitude towards carers who "have let children down", or of simply wanting to protect children from further pain.

> Meryl was a professional woman, who had a five-year-old boy placed with her for adoption. The placement disrupted after three months when Barry disclosed prior sexual abuse and developed unexpectedly extreme behavioural problems. Meryl wanted to maintain contact with Barry but the local authority insisted it would be too upsetting for Barry to be reminded of "the failure". At the disruption meeting, ten weeks later, the new foster carer described how Barry had kept asking to speak to Meryl and she had to explain to him that he wasn't allowed.

If permanency plans disrupt during introductions, prospective carers may feel that they have no right to stay in touch with the child, but if they can be helped to maintain contact, a child may gain a friend instead of having to mark up yet another loss. If family and child have been painstakingly matched, they presumably have something to offer each other, even if it is not a permanent parent–child relationship. Staying in touch can be anything from sending occasional postcards to taking an active interest in the child's future. Whether, why and how to stay in touch should be discussed with the carers and the child as soon as the decision not to proceed with the placement is made. This is essential but often not done.

If disruption happens after a child has been living with the new family for a short time, loss and yet another transition will be inevitable. Families should not only be fully involved in making the transition as painless as possible for the child, but should also be encouraged to take responsibility for minimising the loss. The extent to which they can support the child and sustain a relationship will depend on the placement history and the management of the disruption. At best, the prospective carers and their extended family will continue to play a part in the child's life; at the very least, they should be able to convey to the child that they are still concerned. This could be a time to revive other relationships too. It may be the right time to review the arrangements for contact with the birth family, with previous foster carers, social workers and other significant people who are too often left behind in the move towards permanence.

When an established, apparently stable placement disrupts after a year or more, most often during adolescence, the child's distress may reflect the feelings aroused by the original separation from their birth family. Staying connected to the carers then becomes as important a factor for continuity as remaining in contact with their birth family. In other words, the child will still have two families even if she or he doesn't want to, or can't, live with either. And the second family will probably be as devastated and as much in need of counselling and support as birth families usually are.

Whatever the circumstances of disruption, it is vital to enable children and young people to include the story of the disrupted placement in their own life story, even if they and everyone around them would rather forget. But the child's version of the disruption has to be respected, however much it differs from other accounts.

CASE EXAMPLES

After his placement disrupted, Jonathan, aged six, asked his social worker to write in his life story book that he didn't want to stay with his new mum and dad because he didn't like the wallpaper in his room – but he did like the wallpaper in his previous foster home.

Sonya, aged 11, had to be moved in a hurry when her adoptive parents separated. She had lived with them for two years. The mother left the home and went abroad with a younger birth child and the father was not able to look after Sonya. She stayed briefly with friends of the family until permanent foster carers were found. Sonya had mild learning difficulties and was very confused by the rapid changes in her life. She still thought of the children's home and her key worker as "home and family" and had some frightening memories of her birth parents. Sonya had a life story book but the carefully recorded facts didn't seem to mean much to her. Her new family wrote a story, using Sonya's words and drawings, about Sonya's experiences. It wasn't a literary work, or completely correct, but it helped Sonya to put the disruption in its place, and she asked for it to be read to her over and over again.

12

The impact of disruption

There is no way in which anyone could ever get used to this part of family placement work and a disruption must be considered as part of that work. The agony of all those involved is different every time but no less agonising one time than another. We know, and we assure the family and reassure the child that everyone has tried hard to make it work, wanted it to work, it just cannot work every time. 'But why not this time?' is the angry, defeated, exhausted, accusing, wounded and often mute reproach of the child, the carers and the workers.

THE IMPACT ON THE CHILD

Infants placed for adoption rarely figure in disruption. This guide is mainly concerned with older children, who move into permanent placements with complex histories of neglect or harm and then have to move again contrary to expectations. Inevitably, even if the child has actively wanted the placement to end, it is another experience of abandonment. 'What is it about me that makes everyone give up on me?' is one unspoken question. Or worse, 'I do bad things, therefore I am bad and make people get rid of me'. Or worst of all, 'is it because I'm black, disabled, or just not like everyone else?' When children are being prepared for a permanent placement, they often ask, 'What happens if it doesn't work out?' They need to be assured and reassured that they will always be looked after.

Children react to disruption in a variety of ways.

Case examples

Claire, a confused four-year-old whose placement ended after six months, pretended it never happened; her prospective adopters said she had lived like a stranger in their midst. After the disruption Claire never spoke of the family she had just left; she was compliant in her new short-term foster home and the foster carer described her as 'a very independent, intelligent and capable little girl who is no trouble to look after because she looks after herself'.

The danger is that young, appealing children like Claire may be re-placed quickly in an attempt to secure permanence and avoid drift in care. But Claire needed an intensive and lengthy spell of play therapy before she was ready to trust herself to be parented. She had never dealt with the separation from her birth family, her traumatic memories, and could not acknowledge this most recent disruption.

> Kevin, aged seven, was devoted to his foster family. He had lived with them for nearly two years while his birth mother's mental health deteriorated. The plan for permanence was based on Kevin's capacity to make secure attachments and to transfer them from the foster carers to the adopters. Kevin did not transfer his attachments, nor did he extend them towards his new family who said he was not the boy they had been prepared for. Kevin finally demonstrated his rage by attacking his adoptive mother with a kitchen knife. The placement disrupted after four weeks. He was able to return to his previous foster carers who welcomed him back and expected life with Kevin to resume as before. But Kevin's behaviour was completely changed. He destroyed his toys, he was rude and disobedient, and he was cruel to the younger foster children. After another four weeks, the foster carers reluctantly had to let Kevin go.

Although Kevin agreed that he wanted a "forever family", he could not understand the implications; he could only show his anger and his desperation about the enforced transitions by his behaviour. Unfortunately, he was too hurt to regain his lost trust in his foster carers and they could not risk the safety of their other foster children. Two disruptions close together threw Kevin into an escalating pattern of unacceptable behaviour that would continue until someone heard what he could not express in words.

> Estelle was ten by the time she was placed with her permanent family. She had survived many changes and moves in and out of care. On her way to join her new family, she said to her social worker, 'Next time I'd like a family by the seaside'. The placement lasted for a year but Estelle never wanted to belong and soon decided she was ready to move on. The family struggled to hold her but Estelle made her wishes clear and ever louder: 'Get me out of here'. She was moved to foster carers, was happy and cheerful, and eagerly began to work with her social worker on finding another permanent family.

Some children have had to manage so many transitions that they cannot deal with the idea of permanence. The grass may always be greener in the next family, and their natural resilience enables them to go through life picking up what they need and discarding it when they no longer have a use for it. For children like Estelle, disruption is just one more event in a chain of similar life changes.

The three scenarios above are neither definitive nor comprehensive examples of the impact disruption may have. There will surely be as many variations as there are children and families. But one thing they will most probably all have in common: the impact of disruption will be closely related to the factors leading to disruption and to the way individuals respond in times of trouble. Thus, Claire who had not made sense of her past, could less and less deal with the present or the future; Kevin who had found stability in his foster home was not ready for another move and consequently lost his trust in caring adults; and Estelle, who was resilient enough to withstand many transitions, was not able to invest in permanence.

But some children can move quickly from disruption to a new placement, even if they were devastated by it, like James.

> James was a boy of eight with a rare syndrome, which caused severe facial disfigurement. He lived in a hospital with kind nurses while he underwent seven years of cosmetic surgery. He was desperate to have a family. He was placed with a young couple who felt that the disfigurement was unimportant. After ten weeks, they were mortified to admit that James' appearance had defeated them. James lost all self-esteem and feared he was quite unlovable. He was placed with an experienced foster family to recover and prepare for the next move. But there was no next move because these carers wanted him to stay and to become their son. They understood why he regressed, why he was selfish and desperate for attention. They were wise enough to know that James was counting the days to see if he would be sent away again after ten weeks. Exactly ten weeks to the day, he was drying the dishes after supper and asked, in as casual a voice as a scared eight-year-old can muster, 'Am I alright then?' And he needed his new parents to assure him that he was. (Quoted in Argent, 1983)

THE IMPACT ON CARERS

Permanent carers have been carefully selected, prepared, trained and supported to look after someone else's children. They are aware that there are high expectations of them and they usually have high expectations of themselves. By the time the Form F or Prospective Adopter's Report has been completed, and detailed family histories written, and they have participated in training groups and intimate home studies, given references and been checked by police, health and children's services, and have received agency approval, carers have every right to consider themselves as people who have passed the test to be parents, who can more than manage, who even have something special to offer. How will they then bear to fail children who have already suffered separations and losses? We have to find ways to help them to regain confidence in themselves as well-meaning people and perhaps as parents.

If the partners in a two-parent family were not in complete agreement about ending the placement, will therapy be available for them as a couple?

If potential carers come from minority ethnic groups and the child is of similar ethnicity, they may blame themselves for being disloyal to their community. If the child has a different ethnic heritage, they may blame the difference for the disruption. Either way, they may feel that the cultural aspect has not been addressed, and they will need a worker sensitive to the specific issues that may trouble black/Asian/minority ethnic carers after disruption.

Mixed heritage carers, who can rarely be linked with a child of exactly the same background, may be affected by conflict in the family if the placement doesn't work out. And transracial and intercountry carers and adopters often carry an extra load of guilt if they cannot sustain what they aimed to do against the odds.

A few families try to cope with the disruption by being angry – angry with the social workers for concealing facts, angry with previous carers for not telling the truth, angry with the support services for being unavailable or inappropriate, angry because this was not the child they hoped for. They will want to be heard and still be angry when they come to disruption meetings, but may be comforted to learn that they are not to blame.

Some families have to withdraw to nurse their wounds. They do not want to put their case, to have counselling or to examine the process that led to disruption. They usually find it too painful to keep in any sort of contact with the child. In extreme cases, if they have tried to parent a seriously traumatised child, they may suffer from secondary post-traumatic stress disorder and one or even both of the carers could become physically ill and therefore incapable of looking after a child. It is more difficult to work with these families after disruption, but they are probably in the greatest need of support.

It is possible for families to concentrate on the details, the packing, the medical appointments, the school, and the arrangements for disruption in order to avoid the feelings. They may then collapse after the child has gone, and are surely entitled to an immediate adoption support service.

There is absolutely no evidence that people who cannot become parents to one child or group of children cannot become parents to another. Many carers have gone on from disruption to create a permanent family. After a disruption, there should be a careful review of the adopter(s) in accordance with the Adoption Agencies Regulations 2005 and statutory guidance (England and Wales), the Adoption Agencies (Scotland) Regulations 2009 in Scotland, or the Adoption Regional Policies and Procedures 2010 in Northern Ireland. The review will need to focus on the impact the disruption has had on every adopter. If the possibility of disruption is built in to the preparation and training from the very beginning, then it is easier to accept it as a delay on a journey rather than the journey's end.

THE IMPACT ON THE BIRTH FAMILY

The disruption of a "permanent" placement can feel not only like a rejection of the birth family's child, but also like a condemnation of the birth family itself. It may reactivate resentment about the way social workers have made decisions. It may prompt opposition to future plans for the child or raise hopes of increased contact and rehabilitation. It may possibly reveal family strengths that have hitherto been unknown.

A Family Group Conference after a disruption may produce an offer of kinship care. At the very least, birth families should be told as soon as a placement disrupts and be offered the support to deal with it.

THE IMPACT ON THE SOCIAL WORKERS

> *According to the practitioners in this study...rather than being a culture that fosters openness, an organisational culture of blame is prevalent in children's services, one that fosters a fear of talking about incidents that could have, or actually did, go wrong.* (Bostock *et al*, 2005, p.37)

When thinking about what the impact of a placement disruption might be on professionals, we need to take into account the immense investment of energy and scarce professional time a permanency decision will already have demanded. Helping to decide where a child will live "for ever" will be a process consisting of both personal and professional elements for all the workers and carers concerned. Even to use the phrase "for ever" is to evoke not only the child's perspective on the seeming infinity of future time, but also to recall the perspective of that idealistic earlier self within the worker which found expression in the choice of social work as a career in the first place.

There are a multitude of specifically professional steps that must precede any permanency decision. Though these steps are part and parcel of the normal social work task in family finding, it is difficult to characterise them in purely"professional" language:

- the emergence of the permanence plan and the final discounting of alternatives;
- the battles in court;
- any aspirations to achieve a match comprehensively satisfying all the child's identified needs, while having to bow to the reality of imploding time-scales and narrowing choice;
- the comparative analysis of many potential matches, or maybe if a placement is with the current carer, the preparation of a Form F or Prospective Adopter's Report;
- the distributing of roles and responsibilities;
- meeting families and integrating evidence and intuition to find "the right fit";
- the final entrusting of the child to a named household and its prospective carers, with all their particular history, and that mix of strengths and vulnerabilities characteristic of prospective carers brave enough to take up the challenges we set them;
- the co-ordinating and monitoring of introductions;
- the identification of support resources;
- finally, the watching, and waiting, and sustaining, while not intruding, as the relationship between a child and their new carers develops into a permanent placement or, in spite of all their efforts, ends in disruption.

Trained social workers will probably already have self-selected for resilience and resourcefulness in choosing this as their profession. They will be careful to maintain a child-centred focus if disruption happens, and will have learnt from their wider family work how to avoid being recruited into a partisan role in the enactment of family scripts. They should be aware that their capacity for empathy might make them vulnerable to secondary trauma.

They will need to offset these risks through intelligent use of formal and informal support networks, to include the kind of "trusted challenger" that Kate Cairns (2005) has argued can make an important difference in maintaining well-being: a candid and not uncritical friend. Sometimes what the worker will need is simply support from management, team and panel to help them recover confidence and a sense of belief that they can continue to do the job pretty well, despite the setback of a disrupted placement. In one agency a colleague accompanies them just once or twice as they resume their normal duties of assessing or supporting carers and placements and recover their nerve.

THE INFLUENCE OF ROLE

Social workers' reactions to disruption will also be influenced by the particular role they have undertaken in the child's permanence plan. The family-finding social worker will have been involved in endorsing the adopters' suitability and durability, and after a disruption may be left with a feeling almost of complicity in a wrongdoing, i.e. of seeming to have misjudged the adopter's competence, while also feeling that a valuable "adopter resource" has somehow been misused within the system.

For the child's social worker, the goal of permanence that for a moment seemed all but achieved will have abruptly receded once more; the worker will be left to manage a frustration and anger that the child advocacy dimension of their role almost requires them to articulate. But this will inevitably be in tension with the obligation to empathise with and contain, which is essential to the parental dimension of their role.

ISSUES FOR MANAGERS

Disruption is not something that will have come out of the blue for either the social workers or the managers. Very often a manager will have already been organising additional resources, as they engage in a difficult balancing act of deciding how far to go on shoring up a placement, before reaching the reluctant conclusion that the placement is unsustainable. Will they now be able to disentangle themselves from the immediate dynamics, and focus on supporting the staff involved and the others affected?

A disruption will make workers start questioning the quality of their own assessments and their ability to go on functioning effectively. Managers may have to deal with complicated issues like formal complaints, while they give urgent attention to other aspects of the case, especially to the current and future needs of the child. There may be additional issues when children are removed amid alleged and unresolved child protection concerns.

The combination of external pressures and individually-held reservations about a plan or its implementation can mean that managers get caught up in a maze of self-questioning. Were they aware of concerns – gaps in the adoption support plan, awkward tensions within the professionals' network – without being able to give the time and energy to finding solutions? Were difficulties looming of a kind that made everyone too uncomfortable to ensure they received sustained attention? Was the manager both aware and not aware? We may take in what is happening with one part of our mind, but with another we repudiate what we have seen.

The worst result, for both managers and social workers, is that disruption inhibits openness of case discussion. The kind of help workers may need after a disruption could be made available separately from (and as a preparation for as well as a review after) the disruption meeting itself, either as a one-off debriefing session, or as part of something like an ongoing consultation forum, similar to that recommended for child protection staff in a Demos publication (Cooper *et al*, 2003). Such a forum could provide support, a space for reflection and collaborative challenge, the opportunity to express the valid but often difficult feelings professionals will have after a disruption, and help to develop a shared understanding of the decision-making pattern in any particular case. It can provide a creative counterbalance to the pressures of culture in children's services, which current survey evidence suggests is likely to be risk-averse, target-focused, and distinctly more favourable to action than to organisational learning (Bostock *et al*, 2005).

13
The Chair's reports and minutes

As with any social work intervention, a clear record should be made of the disruption meeting. This will entail arranging for full minutes to be taken. Some agencies will then ask the Chair to append their conclusions and recommendations to the agreed minutes. While that is an entirely valid approach, we would recommend the practice of commissioning a separate, comprehensive report from the Chair. Apart from helping to separate fact from opinion and interpretation, this two-report format gives the Chair more scope to expand on the dominant themes, and to comment on the implications for the child, the family and the agency. (See Appendix 6 for an example of a disruption report.)

MINUTES

An accurate set of minutes of the meeting, capturing as much of the verbatim discussions as possible, will be needed as an objective detailed record.

The purpose of the minutes will be to provide a full account for the agency of everyone's contributions to the meeting, and the Chair's comments and conclusions as expressed in the meeting. In disruption meetings there are often issues that have to be approached sensitively, but cannot be avoided, and indeed should not be avoided, in the minutes. The reasons for actions and decisions in the narrative of the case should have been elicited by the Chair, and should be clearly recorded so that they are available to agency personnel and other people authorised to see the minutes.

Taking minutes is a skill. Minutes of whole day disruption meetings are very long, often 20–30 pages, and an experienced minute-taker will be needed. Some agencies may prefer to split the task between two minute-takers. A minute-taker from the staff team of the agency convening the meeting, or from a consortium involved in the placement, is likely to have the advantage of knowing local procedures and professionals, and may perhaps even be familiar with the case. An external commission may be necessary if no one else with the requisite skills and knowledge is available. Some organisations that can offer independent Chairs can also provide a minute-taker.

Agencies may wish to use disruption meeting minutes for research or other monitoring purposes. In such cases, in order to preserve confidentiality, the minutes should not include surnames or addresses of prospective adopters and carers; children should be referred to by first names or capital letter alone. It is usual to circulate the minutes (agreed by the Chair) to everyone present, but this should be discussed at the beginning of the meeting as many participants prefer to have only the Chair's report.

REPORT

An interpretive overview report should be produced by the Chair of the meeting. The most logical way to structure this will be to follow the sequence of issues set out in the agenda that will have shaped the meeting's proceedings.

In accordance with the principles of good social work recording, the report should differentiate clearly between facts and professional opinions, and opinions will need to be substantiated. The report should be designed as a tool to help those given access to it to reflect upon "why", and not just "what", in the disruption process.

Achieving these purposes is a demanding task for the report writer. The central challenge is to write a report that is faithful to the narrative and dynamics of the disrupted placement, whilst being cast in a format that can be fed back to all the key stakeholders involved in the process and one which promotes learning. The danger is in reports either being too case-specific and detailed for use as a practical tool, or ending up as a one-size-fits-all that is predictable and formulaic.

We suggest that the report should consider the following questions:

- What did the meeting contribute to an understanding of how and why this placement disrupted?
- How far did the meeting provide an opportunity to hear and validate the experiences of all the key participants?
- Did the meeting generate learning points that need to be highlighted, in relation to factors concerning the child, the carers, the agency or any other parties to the disruption?
- Are there action points, either agreed and noted at the meeting, or recommended by the Chair, to be set out for implementation and review?

- Are there implications from the meeting in relation to future planning for the child?
- Has the child's voice been heard directly or been adequately represented?
- To assist planning following a placement disruption, the Chair's report (or the section on conclusions and recommendations should be incorporated into:
  - the child's records;
  - the adopter's or foster carer's report, if they are to be considered for another placement.

Apart from helping with the process of reviewing the work at managerial and agency level, disruption reports will serve a valuable function in helping new workers become familiar with a case, as well as giving a focus to the case supervision.

RECORDING AND UNDERSTANDING CHILDREN'S VIEWS

Whether the child has had an active part in the meeting or not, we would stress the need to ensure that information in relation to a child's views is given particular emphasis in minutes and reports.

Engaging with and communicating with children is an area of practice where agencies struggle. There are many reasons for this: recruitment problems; skill shortages within the children and families workforce; the multiplication of other tasks depriving social workers of time for direct work; and the inherent pain of connecting to the child's experience are just some of these. But the result is that, at present, there are real difficulties in social work practice in ensuring that children's views are understood and taken into account, and accurately conveyed at relevant meetings.

The general advice given by the authors of the training pack, *Write Enough: Effective recording in children's services* (Walker *et al*, 2005) apply to disruption meetings:

> *...it is essential that the views of the child are clearly recorded. In recording the views of children it is important to record when and how those views were expressed. Where different tools have been used to help children express their views, such as drawing or games, their use should be explained. Letters and notes from children, along with drawings can form a legitimate part of the social work record...*
> (www.writeenough.org.uk)

14
Learning from disruption

It would be helpful for agencies to have systems in place to ensure that disruption meetings are regarded as a means by which practice can be reflected upon and improved within the framework of a coherent policy. Otherwise, disruption meetings will risk being no more than sporadic, therapeutic gestures in reaction to placements that have come off the rails. Even a small agency, where disruptions should be comparatively rare events, can devise a route along which lessons can be learnt.

Despite the immediate stresses that will always surround them, disruption meetings can and should be a source of longer-term benefit if agencies have a pro-active approach to learning from disruption. Furthermore, any well-planned disruption meeting will have required a significant investment of resources in terms of agency time and budgets, and only an alert response to the lessons from disruption will justify the time and money spent.

DISRUPTION AND THE ADOPTION AND PERMANENCE PANEL

Ensuring that feedback is received when placements disrupt is clearly an important part of the panel's role. Thus panels should receive reports on all placement disruptions where they have played a part through their recommendations in plans for the child, in approving the adopters or approving the placement. In addition, when considering the cases of children or adopters who have been involved in a previous disruption, adoption and permanence panels should be made aware of the disruption and the views expressed in the Chair's report (or the conclusions and recommendations of the disruption meeting minutes, as the case may be in terms of local procedures).

To strengthen panel involvement and to demonstrate a proper degree of co-responsibility when a disruption occurs, and in order to facilitate subsequent panel discussion on specific placement disruptions, a panel member can be invited to the disruption meeting as an observer. Statistics relevant to disruption should be included in the panel's annual report to the agency.

In order to disseminate what has been learnt from disruption, joint training might be offered for practitioners, managers and panel members, to consider measures for preventing and dealing with disruption in the future. Every agency has the opportunity to develop a training programme directly related to its own experience of disruption. Consortia may profit from pooling that experience. However painful it may be, we will learn more about family placement by careful examination of disruption. It is as important to understand why some placements do not work as it is to rejoice that so many do.

> *However painful the process of disruption inevitably is, it can be viewed as a stage on the path to stability for the child and no one need lose everything.* (Argent, 2003, p.321)

Appendix 1
Reported disruption rates according to age at placement and length of study

Authors	Date	Age placed	Design	Length of study	Disruption rate (%)
Kadushin	1971	6 years+	Retrospective	7 years	10
Trimitiere	1984	6–12 years	Retrospective	4 years	10
		2–18 years			13
Boyne	1984	6–8 years	Retrospective	Not known	15
		9–11 years			25
		12–17 years			47
Barth and Berry	1988	3 years+	Retrospective	4 years	10
Fratter *et al*	1991	'Older'	Retrospective	6 years	21
Borland – Lothian	1991a	Infancy+	Prospective	3 years	21
Borland – Strathclyde	1991b	Infancy+	Retrospective	3 years	43
Rushton *et al*	1988/95	5–9 years	Prospective	8 years	19
Holloway	1997	Infancy+	Retrospective	5 years	20
Quinton *et al*	1998	5–9 years	Prospective	1 year	5
Rushton *et al*	2001	5–11 years	Prospective	1 year	10
Rushton and Dance	2006	5–6 years	Prospective	6.5 years	6
		7–8 years			20–30
		9 years			40–50
Smith *et al*	2006	0–13+	Retrospective	6 years	9
		0–2			9
		2–3			8
		4–6			9
		7–9			9
		10–12			11
		13+			14

Reproduced from *The Adoption of Looked After Children* by Alan Rushton, Social Care Institute for Excellence, 2003

Appendix 2
Sample letters

LETTER TO INVITE FAMILIES

Dear –

As you already know from your social worker, [name], it is this agency's practice to hold a disruption/intervention meeting whenever a child's placement has to end, or is in danger of ending unexpectedly, in order to understand better what has happened and to plan for the future.

I have been asked to convene a meeting regarding [child's name] placement with you, and am writing to invite you to attend. It is important that we make arrangements to suit you and your family; please let me know which days of the week are best for you, whether you plan to go away during the next six weeks or if you need any assistance with travel and child care.

The meeting will be held in the [name] area, and I will send you details of the venue, further information about disruption/intervention meetings and an agenda when we have agreed a date. Meetings usually take the best part of a day; refreshments and lunch will be provided. Your attendance will be very important and greatly valued.

Please do not hesitate to get in touch with your social worker to discuss further, or you can reach me on [phone number].

I look forward to hearing from you.

Yours sincerely

LETTER TO INVITE PROFESSIONALS

Dear –

As you probably know, it is this agency's practice to hold a disruption/intervention meeting whenever a child's placement has to end unexpectedly, or is in danger of ending abruptly, in order to understand better what has happened and to plan for the future.

I have been asked to convene a meeting regarding [name of child/ children] and am initially contacting you in order to find a date to suit all the potential participants. Your contribution to the meeting would be greatly valued, and I would be grateful if you would confirm your interest, and let me know which days of the week are a possibility for you and whether you will be away during the next six weeks.

I will send you further details about the meeting and an agenda as soon as we have agreed a date. These events usually take up a whole day; please let me know if you can only attend for half a day, or if you would prefer to limit your contribution to one specific session. You can reach me to discuss further on [telephone number] or you can email me [email address].

I look forward to hearing from you.

Yours sincerely

CONFIRMATION LETTER TO FAMILIES

Dear –

I am very pleased that you will be able to attend the disruption/ intervention meeting on [date]. I now enclose more information about these meetings from BAAF*, a map of the venue and an agenda. Please let me know if you have any special requirements.

We look forward to seeing you and will do our best to make it a valuable experience for all concerned. Please do not hesitate to contact me, or your social worker, if you have any queries.

Yours sincerely

CONFIRMATION LETTER TO PROFESSIONALS

Dear-

I am very glad that you will be able to attend the meeting regarding [child's name] on [date].

* See Appendix 3.

I enclose a map of the venue, some information about disruption/intervention meetings from BAAF and an agenda. The meeting will be chaired by [name and position held]. Please do not hesitate to contact me if you have any queries or special requirements.

We look forward to seeing you.

Yours sincerely

Appendix 3
Notes sent to all participants before intervention and disruption meetings chaired by BAAF Southern England

These meetings have been an important part of BAAF services since 1977 and have proved to be a valuable and necessary support mechanism. They have also helped us to understand more about why some placements do not work out and to recognise the consequent implications for practice. Meetings may be called in order to consider specific problems within a placement or as an aid to agency thinking and planning either before or after disruption.

Convening one of these meetings is a complex task. It can be daunting for families to attend while struggling with their own feelings about the child and the placement or disruption. Families must know how essential their contribution will be and that, without them, we will not be able to appreciate fully what is happening or has happened. Professionals may also be reluctant to share their knowledge and opinions and to have their practice discussed, but unless everyone concerned with the placement and/or the disruption can attend, invaluable information will be lost. Thorough preparation for an intervention or disruption meeting and support for the people who attend, is therefore crucial.

Many more young people, who are the subject of meetings, are now choosing to attend. So far, experience suggests that, with sensitive preparation, support and chairing, attendance can help some young people to see their situation more clearly and to participate more fully in future planning. If attendance is agreed, young people will have to be fully aware of their own history. It may be useful to arrange a brief, informal meeting with the Chair first.

PURPOSE OF MEETINGS

1. To enable participants to share information and feelings about the placement process, the placement and, if applicable, the disruption. No blame will be attached; all feelings will be acknowledged.
2. To identify issues which have led to difficulties or disruption. Disruption or difficulties are rarely the result of a single factor.
3. To explore and identify the needs of all parties – the child, the adopters, the birth parents and the agency or agencies.
4. To highlight areas for development in practice.

Apart from the carers and their families, all professionals closely involved with the child or children are invited, together with their supervisors. The family's and young person's social workers will spend time with them after the meeting. It is usual also to invite key people from the child's past, especially previous carers. Birth parents or other family members may be able to make a valuable contribution if circumstances allow. When a child from a minority ethnic group is the subject of the meeting, someone who can identify with the child and who is aware of the cultural and religious implications will be present. If anyone is unable to attend the meeting, steps will be taken to ensure that their views are accurately conveyed either in writing or by another member of the group.

It is not possible to predict the exact length of a meeting but a day is usually set aside for the task. Each stage of the meeting is an integral part of the whole, so punctuality is important and, unless absolutely unavoidable, it is not desirable for anyone to attend only part of the meeting.

Meetings take place in informal venues whenever possible, with space for everyone to sit in a circle on comfortable chairs. Tea, coffee, cold drinks, biscuits and lunch will be available.

An agenda will be sent at least one week before each meeting. Social workers should be familiar with the details which the meeting will cover and should bring their files in case further clarification is needed. Visual aids, such as flow charts, may be used.

Attending an intervention/disruption meeting can be a useful training experience but observers may be invited only with the agreement of all the other participants and their number should be limited. An independent Chair will be appointed by BAAF. He or she will not have been involved in the placement and will possess only basic knowledge of the case prior to the meeting and hold no direct responsibility for what happens to the child in the future.

A written report will be sent by BAAF one to two weeks after the meeting. Anonymity will be preserved, but due to the confidential nature of the contents, circulation will be limited to key participants and agreed at the meeting. BAAF can arrange for a minute-taker if requested to do so, but it may be preferable for one of the workers familiar with the case to take notes.

Appendix 4
Jay's moves

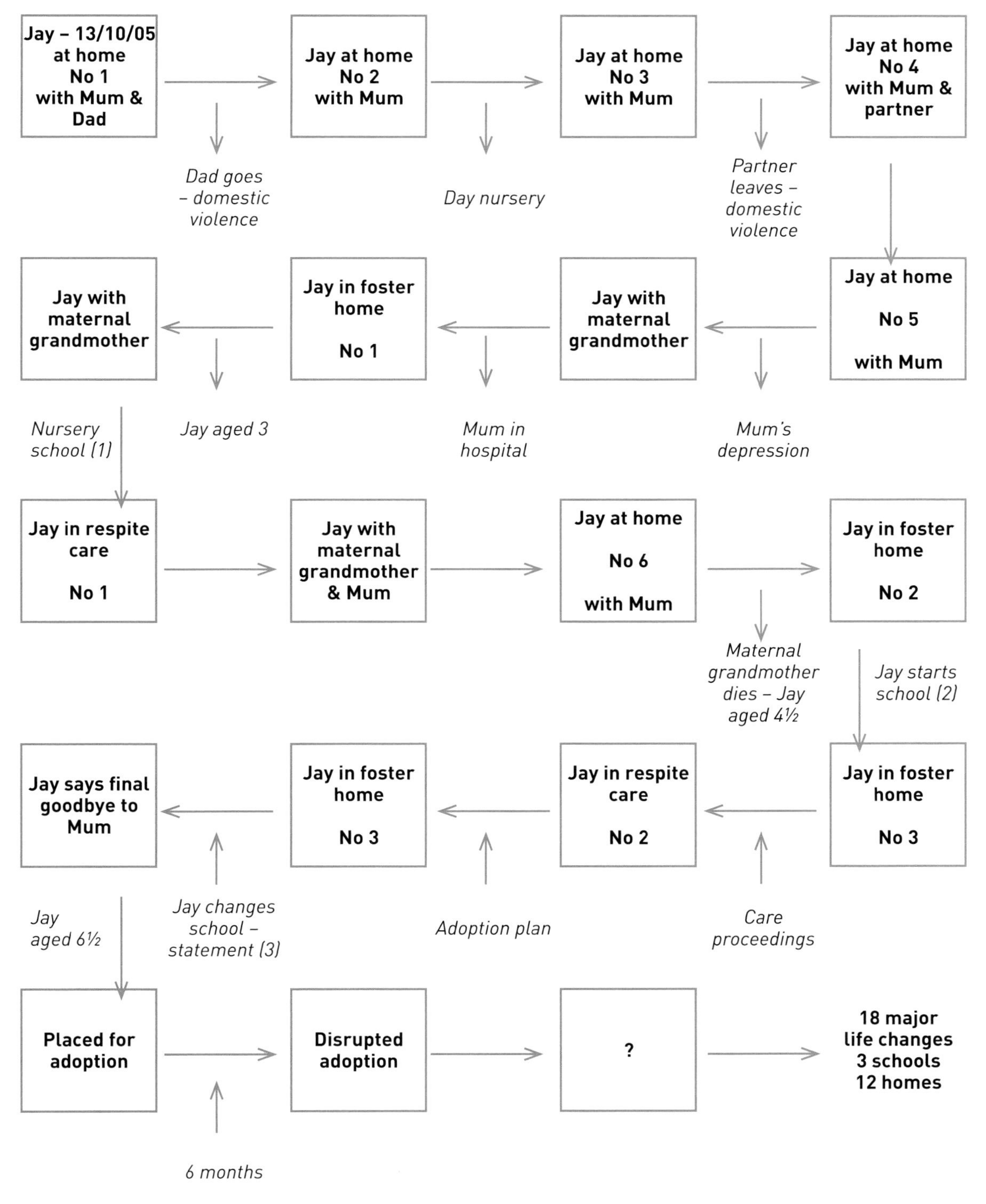

Losses: Jay aged 7

Carers

Foster family 1
Foster family 2
Foster family 3
Respite carer 1
Respite carer 2
Other foster children
Extended foster families
Prospective adopters

Birth family

Mum
Dad
Mum's partner
Maternal grandmother
Extended family

Corporate parent

4 social workers
Teachers (2 schools)
Nursery nurses
Doctors

Appendix 5
Child Appreciation Days

A Child Appreciation Day can be a means of sharing a great deal of information in a relatively short time. It is a day for prospective permanent carers to meet *all* the people who have known or have worked with the child: current and, if possible, previous carers, teachers and social workers. It creates an opportunity for a multi-faceted view of the child to be revealed through anecdotes, diaries, social work records, videos and photographs. The agency's medical, legal and educational advisers should be present for at least part of the day; less official people may also be able to make a significant contribution: a dinner lady, a neighbour or the mother of a playmate might see the child in a different light.

Social workers should produce visual aids on flip charts: family trees and family circles, and flow charts to represent moves, separation and losses can sometimes communicate better than words. A Child Appreciation Day could be described as a guided tour through the child's life, which must always be mindful of how the child sees it.

Such a day works best in a friendly, spacious setting with comfortable chairs arranged informally. Drinks, biscuits and sandwiches for lunch are usually very welcome. As one family put it, 'That day gave us the chance to ask the questions we didn't even know we wanted to ask'.

Adapted from *Ten Top Tips for Placing Children* (Argent H, (2007) London: BAAF)

The Good Practice Guide, *Child Appreciation Days* (Sayers and Roach, 2011, published by BAAF) gives practical information on how to organise, prepare and run a Child Appreciation Day.

Appendix 6
An example of a disruption report

Below is an example of a Chair's report following a disruption meeting. The report is based on factual circumstances but all names and identifying details have been changed.

Introduction

It was always known that Cherry's placement would present a family with more than the usual difficulties. She is a child who makes an impression wherever she goes. She can be very charming; she is academically able; she can be caring. But she can also be verbally and physically aggressive to other children and adults.

Cherry's history, behaviour and needs were well documented and Jill and Steve, the prospective adopters, were as fully informed and prepared as was possible. Cherry had therapeutic support to help her with the transition and was apparently ready to move with her foster carer's approval. Social work support was provided for the family and for the child; the two agencies involved worked closely together. No single event led to the disruption, but after a year Cherry was still unconnected to the family, and Jill and Steve could see no hope for the future. In the event, the ensuing disruption was sensitively planned and managed in painful circumstances.

Cherry at home

Cherry's first two-and-a-half years were spent with her mother, Sylvie, Zoe, her older sister, and with her mother's partner, Dave, who was not the girls' father. Cherry's half-brother James was born a year after Cherry. The children competed fiercely for attention. Home life was marked by violence, neglect and frequent moves. Dave singled out Cherry for punishment and humiliation. Her mother was unable to protect her. There was concern about all the children's basic care and developmental delay, the chaotic relationships in the family, and the risk of abuse.

Sylvie became pregnant when she was 17 and her first son, Daniel, now aged 10, has always lived with Sylvie's mother and stepfather. These grandparents were also significant people in Cherry's life.

Cherry, Zoe and James were accommodated together in April 2004 and placed in emergency foster care for one week, following an escalation of domestic violence at home. Cherry and Zoe were then moved to the foster home where Cherry remained for three years and where Zoe still lives. At the time of the initial assessment for the court, Cherry was described as the most "seriously damaged" child the psychiatrist had seen in 20 years. Aged two-and-a-half, Cherry had no recognisable speech, could not feed herself and cried a great deal; she was weak and puny for her age.

- Sylvie was able to work with social services and the children were accommodated under Section 20 of the Children Act 1989 for one year.

Cherry in foster care

Cherry and Zoe were placed with Hilary, an experienced foster carer and her daughter Juliet. When Cherry came to her, she could not eat proper meals, made herself sick, 'played like a monkey' and had 'dead eyes'. Hilary said that she had never met a child who was so angry; she had serious temper tantrums.

Hilary found ways to manage Cherry's outbursts and could humour her out of her moods. She felt that Cherry retaliated rather than provoked, but that in many situations she experienced ordinary communications as hostile in intent. Hilary found it hard to handle Cherry's competitive relationship with Zoe and was in no doubt that any carer would find Cherry hard work. Cherry bit her nails to the quick and still wet the bed at night when she moved on after three years.

Cherry did very well when she went to school and came top of her class. But the school found her difficult to manage: she wouldn't sit still and she attacked other children in the playground.

At first, Cherry had weekly contact with her mother. During the care proceedings this was reduced to monthly direct contact with her mother, maternal grandmother and half-brother Daniel, although Daniel did not always turn up. Cherry is said to have enjoyed seeing her birth family but her behaviour was worse after visits. She and Sylvie frequently shouted at each other as though they were both children. There was little evidence of a normal parent–child relationship. Cherry also had direct contact with her brother James, who has been adopted. She said, 'James is little, I love him big bits'. Cherry worried whether her mother, who had a new partner, would look after her half-sister, Bella, who was born while Cherry was accommodated.

Cherry was referred for therapy to the local CAMHS; a comprehensive assessment was carried out and it was suggested that therapy would be needed to help Cherry sort out her feelings about her past and her birth family, and help with the transition to adoption when that became the active plan.

Cherry's social worker and foster carer also prepared her for adoption. Cherry has a life story book, which is mainly made up of photographs, but could be added to later to match her growing comprehension. She seemed to understand the difference between fostering and adoption, was aware of the search for a permanent family and seemed to take in the impending separation from birth family and foster family. She is said to have formed secure attachments to Hilary and to Juliet.

- Sylvie did not try to undermine the foster placement.
- Cherry's relationships with the foster family were probably the first secure attachments she had ever made.
- It is unlikely that Cherry, aged five, could grasp the concept of permanence or of permanent separation from her mother or her foster family.

AGENCY PRACTICE

There was inevitable delay in planning Cherry's future because members of the birth family wished to be assessed as kinship carers, and the agency, very properly, carried out this time-consuming task before exploring other routes to permanence. In the event, kinship care was not a possibility and care proceedings were instigated to support a plan for adoption.

It was felt that there was no chance of rehabilitation, that Cherry was young enough for adoption and that she could make further progress. Permanent foster care was not considered because 'local authorities don't make good parents'.

Although it had at first been intended to place all three children together, James by this time had already been adopted, and it was decided that Cherry and Zoe had a negative relationship and 'astonishingly different needs' and should be placed separately.

The prospective adopters for Cherry were recruited through *Be My Parent*. This was an interagency placement and the two agencies co-operated fully. Unfortunately, there was a change of family worker at the time of matching, and the new worker did not have time to read Cherry's files before placement.

Contact arrangements with the birth family were made to meet the court's requirements. Direct contact with them was terminated when Cherry was placed for adoption. There was no formal plan for maintaining continuity with the foster family. Placement support and adoption support were comprehensive and effective.

- The widespread practice of "final visits" with birth family members has to be questioned if we accept that adopted children will always be the children of two families. Children of Cherry's age cannot comprehend or internalise that they will not see their parents again, and they may blame the new parents for having to say "goodbye" to the old.
- Contact arrangements imposed by courts may have to be challenged although this can be difficult. How to maintain continuity for the child must be assessed first, the purpose of contact then has to be clarified, and the arrangements to serve that purpose come last.
- When a child is placed for permanence, it is as well to wait and involve the prospective carers in negotiating contact arrangements to meet their new child's needs.
- Most foster carers have a significant contribution to make in helping a child to settle into an adoptive family. Direct contact in the early stages is often thought to be confusing for the child, but maintaining continuity with previous carers will help rather than hinder the new placement.
- A placement should not proceed until the family's worker has had the opportunity to read all of the identified child's files and considered what implications this information has for the new placement.
- The decision to separate siblings should always be based on an expert assessment of long-term needs rather than on current experience.

PREPARATION OF PROSPECTIVE ADOPTERS

Jill and Steve joined a training group for prospective adopters and found it 'tremendously helpful'. They were linked with other adopters who had an older birth child. Their own daughter, Beth, aged eight, was included appropriately at every stage.

They made the most of their home study in spite of three changes of social workers. They were satisfied with their prospective adopter's report. The family placement worker had commented that Jill would find it hard to parent a child with an attachment disorder.

Jill and Steve pursued their interest in Cherry after seeing her featured in *Be My Parent*. At the time, Jill and Steve felt that they had all the information available about Cherry. They read some reports and met Cherry's therapist and teachers who could help them to understand her.

There was only a brief period between matching and introductions. Although they did not have a Child Appreciation Day, and were not offered the opportunity to read Cherry's files, they met her birth mother and her foster carer and learned more about her from her social worker. They visited her school and her foster home.

They were told that there would be telephone contact with Hilary and Juliet and letterbox contact with Cherry's birth mother and grandmother. They were also hoping to reinstate direct contact with James and his new family.

It was reassuring for Jill and Steve to know that everyone seemed to like Cherry in spite of her problems. They said, 'We knew we would have to start by going backward but we wanted to go'.

- Although their various information-gathering meetings were helpful, a Child Appreciation Day would have been more helpful still to the adopters. Carers say this is an event that gives them the chance to hear conflicting views about the child and the leisure to put questions that they wouldn't otherwise have known they wanted to ask (see Appendix 5).
- If a child's history is recorded in social work files, then prospective permanent carers should be allowed to read them. They may need help to interpret and absorb what has been recorded, and they should feel entitled to return to this source of information at various times during the placement. Adopters who are entrusted with the permanent care of other people's children and who are expected to offer total commitment 24 hours a day have a right to see all the information about their child-to-be.
- In the prospective adopter's report, the social worker clearly commented that Jill would find a child who could not attach most worrying – not for her own sake but for the child's. This does not mean that it was a mistake to place Cherry with the prospective adopters, but perhaps more preparatory work could have been done around unattached behavioural patterns, the underlying feelings, and helpful interventions.
- It is doubtful whether telephone or letterbox contacts are enough to maintain continuity for a young child.
- The time between "matching" and introductions is the most crucial in the placement process. It is when *this* family can be prepared for *this* child, and *this* child for *this* family. Despite everyone's natural enthusiasm to proceed quickly, and despite the pressure exerted by statutory adoption timescales, investment of time and resources at this stage can be a significant factor in avoiding disruption.

INTRODUCTIONS AND PLACEMENT

The introduction plan was agreed by everyone involved. The timing fitted in with the foster family's holiday plans and Jill's adoption leave.

But Cherry went through extreme reactions, which were later mirrored in the placement. A 'magical afternoon' could be followed by a most dismal visit. Cherry could be both 'incredibly winning' and 'incredibly vicious'. Beth, the prospective adopters' daughter, was thumped by Cherry; she didn't know how to deal with that but she wanted to carry on. By the halfway review of introductions, Jill and Steve felt 'shell-shocked' but they were definite that they wanted to keep going.

Apparently, Hilary thought that introductions should be extended, but she didn't say so because the general view was that everyone would feel more positive once the placement was established on the adopters' home ground. Also, postponing the placement date would have meant Cherry going on holiday with the foster family or having a short break in another foster home.

Cherry's school gave her a send-off with an address book to help her remember her friends and teachers. Hilary gave her a family party.

On the day of the move, at the beginning of the Christmas holidays, Hilary and Juliet were in tears but Cherry was not. Jill and Steve were scared, but didn't want to say so in case they seemed uncommitted. Beth was fine and everything went according to plan.

- It might have been reassuring for Cherry to know when and how often she would see Hilary and Juliet again. It can be comforting to put the emphasis on continuity during introductions, rather than on making a new start.
- It is important to ensure that everyone is heard during introductions. The foster carer, who was in the best position to judge how Cherry was doing, did not feel she could voice her doubts; the prospective carers could not say they were scared. A delay might have been helpful but everyone felt under pressure to keep to a schedule that was more determined by the complications around the plans of all the various adults than it was by the needs of the child.
- Cherry's lack of distress at moving could have been seen as a danger signal and might have provided a useful trigger to think afresh about attachment patterns in relation to this specific placement.

THE ADOPTION PLACEMENT

There was no "honeymoon period", but there were some early rewards. Cherry showed a sense of humour and, in the right mood, was 'fun to be with' and could be 'wonderful company' because she was amazingly articulate for her age and capable of holding long conversations. Like the rest of her new family, she enjoyed the countryside; she connected with the animals straight away, and contrary to expectations she was even protective towards one of the dogs on her very first day. Her new maternal grandparents were delighted with her.

But, from the beginning, Cherry's difficulties emerged hand in hand with the rewards. Her high expectations of herself caused her to become easily frustrated and to "lose it". For instance, she wanted to ride her bike, wasn't very good at it, and was overcome by anger. She could be charming one minute and spoil the day in the next.

Cherry's carefully planned introduction to her new school was awful. She made it clear from day one that she didn't want to be there. The teachers said that they had never met a child like Cherry before; she would "take on anybody". It was decided that Cherry should only attend for half-days.

Although Cherry was more contented at home than at school to begin with, she soon made it clear to her parents that she didn't want to be with them either. 'She said that she hated us, asked why we chose her, and said that she didn't want to be adopted. She made us feel from the start that we were the wrong family for her.'

Jill and Steve were overwhelmed by 'how destructive it felt'. They couldn't identify triggers for the "shutting-out" behaviours; Cherry went "dead behind the face" without apparent external reasons. She did not want to enter the family circle and was uninterested in the family stories. On one occasion, without apparent cause, she packed her bags to go back to the foster home. Cherry's behaviour controlled the family. Her relationship with Beth was erratic; sometimes the girls played well together but Beth found it increasingly difficult at school. She felt responsible for Cherry although her parents assured her that she was not.

Cherry also seemed to control her continuing therapy at CAMHS. She managed to avoid the painful areas she did not want to explore. It was presumed that her therapist would help her to adjust to her new placement and to manage her feelings about loss and separation. When the therapy ended as planned, Cherry showed no sadness, although she had made a seemingly close relationship with the therapist. Jill and Steve hoped that the end of therapy would herald a better phase but it did not.

However, there was one quite startling improvement. While things got worse at school, Cherry, of her own accord, stopped biting her nails and bed-wetting. She seemed to be exhibiting the strength of her power to control.

Cherry spoke of her birth family and frequently looked at the photos in her life story book. She mentioned James, Daniel and Zoe and said that 'Daddy David was cruel'. She did not speak of her birth mother. Jill and Steve thought that she was missing Hilary and Juliet, who were keeping in touch by telephone, but more often than not Cherry refused to speak to them.

Cherry grew strong and gained weight while in this placement but remained small for her age. She was never ill but appeared to be 'hyper-vigilant', 'worried, not trusting and never relaxing'. Jill and Steve feared that that Cherry was "losing out" because not only was she not maintaining the steady progress she had been making in her foster placement, but she was getting worse day by day.

Jill and Steve enjoyed good support from both agencies. The social workers felt that the adopters were struggling with a child with serious attachment problems but that, despite her traumatised start, Cherry was resilient, and as she had previously shown an ability to attach, would do so again.

- It may have been possible to help Beth more by linking her with other birth children of adoptive families.
- It seems that the more out of control of her life Cherry felt, the more she had to exert control where she could. The relationship between feeling powerless and tyranny was presumably explored in therapy, but the prospective adopters might have been helped by a therapeutic approach that included them as part of the solution to Cherry's problems.
- The concept of helping a child to extend existing attachments rather than to transfer them may ease the transition between foster family and adoptive family, and prepare the way for continuity rather than fragmentation.
- The concept of a "forever family" may feel more like a threat than a promise to children who have not emotionally separated from their birth family or previous carers; it may feel to them like being asked to communicate in a language they do not understand.
- It is common for progress in foster care not to be replicated in a permanent placement. It is often easier for children to do well in less intense family situations where they are not at the centre of everyone's attention.

THE DISRUPTION

No specific event led to the disruption. It was more like the realisation, after nearly a year, that nothing was improving or would improve. Jill and Steve could not discover any way of dealing with Cherry's 'shutting down'. Cherry would not talk to Jill for days and would also shut out Steve if he talked to her. They began to lose sight of 'anything likeable about her'. She could change her behaviour from one moment to the next: she could confound them by being charming while her social worker visited and withdrawing the moment she left. She would physically shut herself away from the family by reading in her room. She showed no affect when the prospective adopters or the grandparents came and went. She would laugh inappropriately if any member of the family was hurt or upset.

Jill and Steve feared that the situation was unhealthy for Cherry, they were worried about the effect on Beth, and they lost all hope for change. They felt that they didn't know how to help or how to limit the damage to themselves.

The disruption was planned and went according to plan. Jill and Steve agreed to keep Cherry until a suitable placement could be found. Jill told Cherry that she would be leaving after she had a particularly prolonged 'screaming fit'. Cherry said that she wanted to stay and tried to be 'very good', but nothing changed: there were 'the usual ups and downs, nothing different'. Cherry did not ask to go back to Hilary and her family. She knew Hilary was expecting another baby.

Cherry was told that Jill and Steve couldn't help her to be happy and that her social worker would find her a family where she could be happier.

It had been a difficult year for Beth and she was partly relieved that Cherry would be going.

Steve met the new foster carers, Christine and Derek, at a meeting to plan the move and could then tell Cherry about them. The carers met Cherry once before she moved. On the day of the move, four weeks after the decision to end the placement, Cherry did not show any emotion on leaving but was excited about going somewhere new. On arrival she went straight upstairs to examine her room. The carers' son, Ian, aged 13, said that Cherry had tears in her eyes, but did not cry.

The social workers supported the disruption as completely as they had supported the placement. They felt what had to be, had to be. Jill and Steve made it clear that they wanted to continue to act in Cherry's best interests and did not wish to cut off from her, but no firm plans were made or future arrangements suggested.

- The prospective carers and the agencies involved should be congratulated on giving thought to planning for the disruption as much as for planning introductions. Both transitions were life-changing for Cherry, but the process of disruption is seldom given enough attention. Perhaps there could have been more visits before the move to the new family.

- After a year with no direct contact, Cherry might have felt abandoned by Hilary, especially as she was having a new baby. Her birth mother was also expecting another child. Cherry had already been replaced by Bella in her birth family, and she may have felt increasingly weighed down with fears of displacement and further losses.
- Jill and Steve's wish to remain connected to Cherry could perhaps have been more formally and creatively pursued. It is difficult for adopters to be assertive in these circumstances and there is a danger that more continuity will be lost. Cherry's life, so far, must seem to her like a series of disconnected episodes.

MOVING ON FROM DISRUPTION

Cherry has been living with Christine and Derek for three months. This is a "parallel planning" placement provided and supervised by an independent fostering agency. Cherry will be able to stay as long as it takes to find a permanent family for her. She is being featured in *Be My Parent* and in *Adoption Today.* The Care Plan is still for adoption but permanent foster care with the right family would be considered. It is thought important for Cherry to be the only child in the family.

The foster carers say that they are able to manage Cherry and that she has improved a lot during the last three months. However, her behaviour does not seem to have changed greatly. She still withdraws, is aggressive, especially towards Christine, laughs inappropriately at others (Ian broke his ankle recently and Cherry laughed although the carers say she was really upset) and she can spoil family events and outings. When she is "good" at home, she is "bad" at school, and vice versa. When she shuts off, she says she doesn't want to talk about it, that it is a secret and that she doesn't want any help. Even so, Christine and Derek like Cherry, and are pleased to have her.

Cherry has already changed schools three times and is about to move from the Infants to the Juniors. She has been lucky to find a head teacher who is taking a special interest in her and is able to work with the foster carers and the local authority. This teacher was concerned enough to attend the whole disruption meeting and to make valuable contributions. Cherry shows more of her feelings at school; she can cry and get upset and she will talk to the head teacher about her moods.

Cherry now talks to Hilary and Juliet on the phone and also to Zoe. She has asked to see her mother, who has had the baby, and Hilary. She misses Beth. Her new social worker is doing more life story work with Cherry and has set up a letterbox for cards to and from her birth family. Jill and Steve have also sent cards. Direct contact with the birth family has not been ruled out but Cherry's birth mother and grandmother are competing with each other and seem to be trying to meet their own needs rather than Cherry's.

Hilary has expressed an interest in becoming a permanent carer for Cherry. This is complicated because she still has Zoe. She is waiting for Zoe to be moved but this is unconnected to Cherry coming. In the meantime, direct contact has not been re-established.

Jill and Steve are recovering but remain saddened by the experience of trying to parent Cherry. It was hard for them to come to the disruption meeting but they shared their feelings and perceptions most generously. They have decided not to pursue adoption further. They hope to remain in touch with Cherry.

Beth still thinks and talks about Cherry. She understands that her parents will not consider adopting any other children. Cherry has become part of the family story – when Beth knew that her parents were going to the disruption meeting, she asked whether Cherry would be coming back. Jill and Steve say that sharing her life and home with Cherry was not all negative for Beth, and that she has learned a lot from it.

Jill's parents were sad about the disruption but relieved that the pressure could be lifted from the family.

Sylvie is managing to look after both her youngest children. She has real support from their father and from his extended family. She has successfully attended a parenting programme and has now become a befriender for other needy mothers. The only other birth family members in the picture are Sylvie's parents, who were important to Cherry when she lived at home.

The agencies have continued to work together after the disruption, and the meeting was proof of their co-operation. However, as is endemic in adoption services, there is never enough time to do everything that should be done, and there was little preparation of all the parties before the disruption meeting.

- It is good to know that a permanent family is still being sought for Cherry. Long-term fostering, with direct contact with significant people, could be easier for Cherry to accept than another adoptive placement, and foster carers can always apply to adopt later.
- It may be better not to be prescriptive about the kind of family Cherry needs. Surprising people can prove to be the right family for a specific child if they are invited in, rather than weeded out, at an early stage.

- The whole area of direct contact for Cherry could perhaps be tackled afresh. What does she want and need? What would be the purpose of each connection? How can the best arrangements be made?
- Cherry is going to need long-term therapeutic help. Ideally she should have help now to prepare her for another transition and she and the new family will need continuing help to make a permanent placement work. The therapy would have to be specifically geared to enabling the whole family.
- "Public parenting" can be daunting in the most advantageous circumstances. Jill and Steve may be able to help other prospective adopters to grapple with these issues.
- Sylvie has apparently not tried to intervene in Cherry's placements. She is at present being a "good enough" mother. She may yet have a contribution to make to Cherry's future.
- A disruption meeting can only be as good as the preparation for it and the follow-up. Can the meeting have a positive impact on Cherry's future? It is usually helpful for all the workers to get together two to four weeks after a disruption meeting to monitor progress and share reactions.
- Other children play a major role in Cherry's story. Juliet, Beth and Ian have been affected by Cherry's placements with their families. Zoe and James have been separated from Cherry. Daniel has always been in the background. Bella and a new baby have taken Cherry's place in her birth family. All nine children might be considered when contact for Cherry is negotiated.

SUMMARY

The recurring themes in this meeting were separation, loss, continuity, the purpose of contact, the use of therapy, and disordered attachments. The bullet points at the end of each section point to practice issues and suggest recommendations that should be further discussed and considered.

This disruption was surely unavoidable given the particular circumstances, but Cherry is a resilient child and many people have said that it is hard not to like her and to respond to her. She is still only seven-and-a-half years old, and with therapeutic help could spend the rest of her childhood in a permanent family.

Chair of disruption meeting

References

Argent H (1983) *Find me a Family*, London: Souvenir Press

Argent H (2002) *Staying Connected*, London: BAAF

Argent H (ed) (2003) *Models of Adoption Support: What works and what doesn't*, London: BAAF

Argent H (2006) *Ten Top Tips for Placing Children*, London: BAAF

Argent H (2008) *Ten Top Tips for Placing Siblings*, London: BAAF

Argent H and Kerrane A (1997) *Taking Extra Care*, London: BAAF

Barn R (2000) 'Race, ethnicity and transracial adoption', in Treacher and Katz (eds) *The Dynamics of Adoption: Social and personal perspectives*, London: Jessica Kingsley Publishers

Barth RP and Berry M (1988) *Adoption and Disruption: Rates, risks, and responses*, New York: Aldyne de Gruyter

Barth RP and Berry M (1991) 'Preventing adoption disruption', *Prevention in Human Services*, 9:1, pp 205–222

Barth RP and Brooks D (2000) 'Outcomes for drug-exposed children, eight years post-adoption', in Barth R P, Freundlich M and Brodzinsky D (eds) *Adoption and Prenatal Alcohol And Drug Exposure: Research, policy and practice*, Washington DC: Child Welfare League of America and The Evan B Donaldson Adoption Institute

Berry M (1997) 'Adoption disruption', in Avery RJ (ed) *Adoption Policy and Special Needs Children*, Westport, CT: Auburn House

Biehal N, Ellison S, and Sinclair I (2010) *Belonging and Permanence: Outcomes in long-term foster carer and adoption*, London: BAAF

Bostock L, Bairstow S, Fish S and Macleod F (2005) *Managing Risks and Minimising Mistakes in the Services to Children and Families: Report 6*, London: Social Care Institute for Excellence

Boyne J, Denby L, Kettenring JR and Wheeler W (1984) *The Shadow of Success: A statistical analysis of outcomes of adoption of hard-to-place children*, Westfield, NY: Spaulding for Children

Brodzinsky DM (2005) 'Reconceptualising openness in adoption: implications for research and practice', in Brodzinsky DM and Palacios J (eds) *Psychological Issues in Adoption: Research and practice*, Westport CT: Praeger

Brodzinsky DM, Schechter MD and Henning RM (1992) *Being Adopted: The lifelong search for self*, New York: Bantam Doubleday

Cairns K (2005) PowerPoint Presentation for BAAF

Cooper A, Hetherington R, Katz I (2003) *The Risk Factor: Making the child protection system work for children*, London: Demos

Cousins J (2006) *Every Child is Special: Placing disabled children for permanence*, London: BAAF

Dance C and Rushton A (2005) 'Predictors of outcome for unrelated adoptive placements made during middle childhood', *Child & Family Social Work*, 10:4, pp. 269–280

Dance C, Rushton A and Quinton D (2002) 'Emotional abuse in early childhood: relationships with progress in subsequent family placement', *Journal of Child Psychology and Psychiatry*, 43:3, pp. 395–407

Department for Education (2011) *Adoption Statutory Guidance*, London: Department for Education

Department for Education and Skills (2005) *Adoption and Children Act 2002 (England and Wales): Statutory Guidance*, Chapter One – Adoption Agency Arrangements, London: Department for Education and Skills

Department of Health (2001) Local Authority Circular LAC (2001) 33, available at www.dfes.gov.uk/adoption/lac200133.shtml, London: Department of Health

Department of Health (2002) *Providing Effective Adoption Support*, London: Department of Health

Donley K (1981) 'Further observations on disruption', in US Department of Health and Human Services, *Adoption Disruptions*, Washington DC: US Department of Health and Human Services

Donley Zeigler K (1996) *The Roundtable*, 10:1, available at www.nrcadoption.org/resources/roundtable/V10N1.pdf

Edwards R, Hadfield L and Mauthner M (2005) *Children's Understanding of their Sibling Relationships*, London: National Children's Bureau in association with JRF

Erich S and Leung P (1998) 'Factors contributing to family functioning of adoptive children with special needs: a long-term outcome analysis', *Children and Youth Services Review*, 20, pp. 135–150

Evan B Donaldson Adoption Institute (2004) *What's Working for Children: A policy study of adoption stability and termination, referring to several studies*, New York, NY: Evan B Donaldson Adoption Institute, available at www.adoptioninstitute.org/publications/Disruption_Executive_Summary.pdf

Festinger T (2005) 'Adoption disruption: rates, correlates, and service needs', in Mallon G and McCartt Hess P (eds) *Child Welfare for the Twenty-First Century: A handbook of practices, policies and programs*, New York, NY: Columbia University Press, pp. 452–468

Festinger T and Maza P (2009) 'Displacement or post-adoption placement? A research note', *Journal of Public Child Welfare*, 3, pp. 275–286

Fitzgerald J (1983, 1990) *Understanding Disruption*, London: BAAF

Glidden L M (2006) 'My child, my choice: parental well-being in the adoption of children with developmental disabilities', in Wegar K (ed) *Adoptive Families in a Diverse Society*, New Brunswick, NJ: Rutgers University Press

Groze V (1996) *Successful Adoptive Families: A longitudinal study of special needs adoption*, Portsmouth, NH: Greenwood Publishing Group

Hegar R (2005) 'Sibling placement in foster care and adoption: an overview of international research', *Children and Youth Services Review*, 27:7, pp. 717–739

Hodges J, Steele M, Hillman S, and Henderson K (2003) 'Mental representations and defenses in severely maltreated children: a story stem battery and rating system for clinical assessment and research applications', in Emde RN, Wolf DP and Oppenheim D (eds) *Revealing The Inner Worlds Of Young Children. The Macarthur story stem battery and parent–child narratives*, New York, NY: Oxford University Press Inc

Howard JA and Smith SL (2003) *After Adoption: The needs of adopted youth*, Washington DC: Child Welfare League of America

Howe D, Brandon M, Hinings D and Schofield G (1999) *Attachment Theory: Child maltreatment and family support*, Basingstoke: Macmillan

Ivaldi G (2000) *Surveying Adoption: A comprehensive analysis of local authority adoptions 1998–1999 (England)*, London: BAAF

Leung P and Erich S (2002) 'Family functioning of adoptive children with special needs: implications of familial supports and child characteristics', *Children and Youth Services Review*, 24:11, pp. 700–816

Lord J and Borthwick S (2008) T*ogether or Apart? Assessing brothers and sisters for permanent placement*, London: BAAF

Lowe N and Murch M (1999) *Supporting Adoption*, London: BAAF

Macaskill C (2002) *Safe Contact? Children in permanent placement and contact with their birth relatives*, Lyme Regis: Russell House Publishing

Mather M (2004) 'Finding out about the past to understand the present: working with the medical adviser in adoption and foster care', in Phillips

R (ed) *Children Exposed to Parental Substance Misuse: Implications for family placement*, London: BAAF, pp. 15–29

McCroy RG (1999) *Special Needs Adoptions: Practice issues*, New York, NY: Garland Publishing Inc

Neil E (1999) 'The sibling relationships of adopted children and patterns of contact after adoption', *Adoption & Fostering*, 23:1, pp. 59–60

Parker R, Ridgeway J and Davies C (eds) (1999) *Adoption Now: Messages from research*, Chichester: John Wiley & Sons

Partridge S, Hornby H and MacDonald T (1986) *Learning from Adoption Disruption: Insights for practice*, Portland, ME: University of Southern Maine Centre for Research and Advanced Study

Pollock S and Farmer E (2005) 'A hidden population: understanding the needs of sexually abused and abusing children in substitute care', *Adoption and Fostering*, 29:2, pp. 18–32

Prevatt Goldstein B and Spencer M (2000) *"Race" and Ethnicity: A consideration of issues for black, minority ethnic and white children in family placement*, London: BAAF

Quinton D (2012) *Rethinking Matching in Adoptions from Care: A conceptual and research review*, London: BAAF

Quinton D, Rushton A, Dance C and Mayes D (1998) *Joining New Families: A study of adoption and fostering in middle childhood*, Chichester: Wiley

Rosenthal JA (1993) 'Outcomes of adoption of children with special needs', *The Future of Children*, 3:1, pp. 77–88

Rushton A (2003) *The Adoption of Looked After Children: A scoping review of research*, London: Social Care Institute for Excellence

Rushton A and Dance C (2004) 'The outcomes of late permanent placements: the adolescent years', *Adoption & Fostering*, 28:1, pp. 49–58

Rushton A and Dance C (2006) 'The adoption of children from public care: a prospective study of outcome in adolescence', *Journal of the American Academy of Child and Adolescent Psychiatry*, 45, pp. 877–883

Rushton A, Dance C, Quinton D and Mayes D (2001) *Siblings in Late Permanent Placements*, London: BAAF

Ryburn M (1994) *Open Adoption: Research, theory and practice*, Aldershot: Ashgate

Sanders R (2004) *Sibling Relationships: Theory and issues for practice*, London: Palgrave Macmillan

Saunders H and Selwyn J (2011) *Adopting Large Sibling Groups: The experiences of adopters and adoption agencies*, London: BAAF

The Scottish Office (1997) *Scotland's Children: The Children (Scotland) Act 1995, regulations and guidance*, Volume 3: Adoption and Parental Responsibilities Orders, Edinburgh: HMSO

Selwyn S, Quinton D, Harris P, Wijedasa D, Nawaz S and Wood M (2010) *Pathways to Permanence for Black, Asian and Mixed Ethnicity Children*, London: BAAF

Smith S (1994) *Learning from Disruption*, London: BAAF

Smith SL and Howard JA (1994) 'The impact of previous sexual abuse on children's adjustment in adoptive placement', *Social Work*, 39:5, pp. 491–501

Thoburn J, Norford L and Rashid SP (2000) *Permanent Family Placement for Children of Minority Ethnic Origin*, London: Jessica Kingsley Publishers

Treacher A and Katz I (eds) (2000) *The Dynamics of Adoption: Social and personal perspectives*, London: Jessica Kingsley Publishers

Walker S, Shemming D and Cleaver H (2005) 'The child is "missing" from the record', in the interactive training pack *Write Enough: Effective recording in children's services*, London: Department for Education and Skills, available at www.writeenough.org.uk/pitfalls_for_practitioners_2.htm

Legal references

England

Statutory Instrument 2005 No. 389
The Adoption Agencies Regulations 2005
Statutory Instrument 2005 No. 691
The Adoption Support Services Regulations 2005

Scotland

Scottish Statutory Instruments 2009 No. 154 The Adoption Agencies (Scotland) Regulations 2009
Scottish Statutory Instruments 2009 No. 152 The Adoption Support Services and Allowances (Scotland) Regulations 2009
Scottish Statutory Instruments 2009 No. 210 The Looked After Children (Scotland) Regulations 2009

Northern Ireland

Adoption Regional Policy and Procedures 2010
The Adoption (Northern Ireland) Order 1987
The Adoption Agencies Regulations (Northern Ireland) 1989

The Children (Northern Ireland) Order 1995
The Children Order (1995) Guidance and Regulations Volume 3, *Family Placements and Private Fostering*

Wales

Welsh Statutory Instrument 2005 No. 1313 (W.95)
The Adoption Agencies (Wales) Regulations 2005
Welsh Statutory Instrument 2005 No. 1512 (W.116)
The Adoption Support Services (Local Authorities) (Wales) Regulations 2005